#IFJOBHADTWITTER

When Hardship Hits The Palace

JEFF GRENELL

ISBN: 1546819010
ISBN 13: 9781546819011
Library of Congress Control Number: 2017913130
CreateSpace Independent Publishing Platform
North Charleston, South Carolina

My Broken Palace

See, in America we all live in a broken palace. A place for beauty and beast. Of more and least. Where princes, princesses, kings, queens, – where dragons, and jesters all meet.

Where a frog is turned into a prince. Where princesses find slippers and princes to marry forever after. Well, that's how the story goes.

My Broken Palace

You know how the story goes. We write new scenes to introduce our old lives. We cover rusted gates with paint. We fix broken arms with Band-Aids. We beautify pigs with dresses. But you know they are still rusted gates, broken arms, and ugly pigs.

My Broken Palace

Where Rapunzel wonders what it's really like outside the castle. Letting down her hair for a prince to rescue her from her despair. It may look like a castle, but nobody sees the hassle the struggle the tussle.

It may look like a palace, but nobody sees the malice, the loss, or the dross. 'Cuz we all live behind the moat and the wall. Behind the shrubs and the facade of the castle, it's not what it seems. The marquee isn't saying who's really playin'. Not for real. It's surreal.

My Broken Palace

Where we sweep our brokenness under the rug, put it in the closet, or say we don't really have it. We ignore what we know is there for all to see. That we hate each other and the weather. Get upset with our neighbor or a brother. We tell each other, "You're a bother." Our parents to shut up 'cuz we're fed up. 'Cuz we sweep our brokenness under the rug and keep it in the closet.

My Broken Palace

Since hardship and trial are part of Christianity and Scripture, why are we so upset about hardship and trial in Christians and culture?

We act like it shouldn't touch us or it shouldn't be us. Not in the US. And not in my palace.

But this mansion, our bastion of hope and ultimate future, is where the pain becomes His platform. Where the mess becomes His message. Where the chaos is placed on His canvas. Where the tragedy becomes His triumph. Where ruins are redeemed and turned into rewards.

My Broken Palace
A palace where the king lives in His castle to rule. Where kings are crowned and queens are wed. Who birth princes and princesses who live in broken palaces. Who slay dragons.

—A Spoken Word by Jeff Grenell

OUTLINE

All scriptures are from the New King James version of the Bible

PREFACE

It all began in the fall of 1981. Some people never find what I found. Walking onto my college campus on the first weekend of school, I saw her. She was walking down the center of campus. I was with an older student in my dorm room, looking out the window, when I saw her.

Turning to my friend, I said to him, "I'm going to marry that girl."

He looked out the window at the girl walking down the middle of campus. Then he turned to me and said, "No, you're not. That's Jane, and you don't have a chance."

The following week, I found out she was on my sister floor, and we would be seeing a lot of each other. As a matter of fact, she went to my first football game with her sister floor and fell in love with my "chicken legs," as she tells it.

On the second weekend of school, I walked into the cafeteria and saw her sitting at a table with her friends. Walking through the line, I kept my eye on her to make sure she didn't leave before I was seated. At her table.

Noticing she had a couple of seats left at her table, my friend and I sat down with these strangers. And this is when my personality kicked into high gear. Looking at Jane in front of all of her friends, I sat down next to her and introduced myself.

And then I asked, "What's your name?"

She replied, "Jane." And she promptly continued eating her meal without looking at me. I knew right there that she liked me.

My reply was confident. "Great to meet you, Jane. Do you know that you are the second girl I've met here at college, and two is my lucky number?"

Needless to say, the whole table was in disbelief. I still don't believe I said that. But I didn't back down. The chances of that working were pretty low. But in that conversation at our first lunch, I did find out where Jane went to church. And I felt called to that church the coming weekend. I made sure to sit right in front of her and her friends. That morning I worshiped like I had never worshiped in my life. And after the service I asked her for a date, and we went to church that evening.

We dated for the next thirty-four years. Thirty-one of those years, we were married. We had three children and a grandchild and were in youth ministry together for thirty-one years. We built a youth ministry from the ground up. We pastored hundreds of students in a mega church, we planted a very young youth church, we travelled the country doing mobile youth work for five years, and we taught youth majors in ministry and development at the university level for ten years. Recently we created a youth leadership organization for the study of youth called *ythology* in the fall of 2015.

And that is where it all ended. Some people never find what I lost.

December 18, 2015, as we were beginning this new organization, Jane passed away after battling cancer for the previous sixteen months. It rocked our Western mind-set that viewed our marriage as near perfect and our family as untouchable. We really had only known harmony as a couple, satisfaction with our kids, and fulfillment with our work.

This is where I had the firsthand glimpse of *My Broken Palace*. At the time, I first began to think that if the Lord tarried, I would not have my best friend to speak with daily, our dates that we made public lessons out of on social media would never happen again, I would never kiss her again, my last child would not have his mother at his wedding, our grandchildren would not know their grandmother, and Jane would not enjoy the fruit of our newly formed organization after more than thirty years of work together.

I mean, we have all changed so much. She would never know the man of God I have become through this season in my life. No doubt that her impact is indelibly marked on our family. And the story of her life will be retold as long as we have a chance. And no doubt that the daily build and early work of our new ministry is a testament to her selfless work in youth ministry. But her death changed everything.

For the first time in my life since I saw her walking on that campus thirty-four years ago, now things would be different. Some people never find what I lost. I did get to marry my best friend, raise three amazing children and a grandchild, and work with thousands of youth over four decades. But her death changed everything.

And this book is the rest of the story on how to deal with hardship, suffering, and loss for all of us.

INTRODUCTION

Sometimes *unlearning* is as important to us as *learning*. Along the way, we gather information about life. And much of that information becomes part of our thinking and behavior. The gathered information may be personal experiences, truths and untruths, peer thought, education, or media influences about everything in life. All of this data shapes how we think about politics, athletics, entertainment, theology, and even ourselves. And we form our opinions and attitudes of what is right or wrong with all of this information. Think about that. Where are you getting your information from? What is shaping your thought? All of that information is shaping your life.

For instance, let's say you live in America. And for this, you feel entitled or special. We have a certain way that we think in the Western world. And if we live in America, never does hardship seem right or even welcomed in our life. We act like it shouldn't touch us. It shouldn't be us, not in the U.S. And not in my Palace. And because of this, we can become entitled to freedoms and blessings or rights that we think we deserve. However, a thorough look at culture will prove that the presence of hardship is necessary, if not useful.

Many of us think that we are immune to difficulty because we are American. In the pages to come, contrary to popular opinion, you will find that culture promotes hardship as a way to maturity and strength. You will see that culture in many ways promotes the productive role of hardship in soldiers, athletes, and farmers. And we are probably okay with that. As long as it is not personal.

In the same way, let's say you are Christian. And for this, you feel entitled or special. We have a certain way that we think in the Western church. And if we are Christian, never does hardship seem right or even welcomed in our life. We act like it shouldn't touch us, it shouldn't be us, not in the church, and not in my palace.

Many of us think that we are immune to difficulty because we are Christian. In the pages to come, contrary to popular opinion, you will find that Christianity promotes hardship as a way to maturity and strength. You will see that Christianity in many ways promotes the productive role of hardship in soldiers, athletes, and farmers (2 Timothy 2.4–6). And we are probably okay with that. As long as it is not personal.

Many authors and researchers, including Kinnaman, Lyons, Barna, Burns, LiveScience, and Howe and Strauss, to name a few, have written about the traits or characteristics of this generation. Most of the traits are negative and tend toward an elitism or specialness that has crippled the younger generation to accepting hardship or difficulty. They just don't have time or thought for crisis or suffering. And because of feeling this way as Americans or Christians, we can become entitled to freedoms and blessings or rights we think we deserve.

This way of thinking comes from an elitism that will not allow difficulty or suffering into our lives. We believe that hardship is injustice. And this cognitive panacea (thinking perfectly) becomes one of the things we must unlearn. Why? It is not true. Hardship and suffering are part of life. Call it free will, accidents, the human condition, or sin, hardship, suffering, and pain are part of the way of life. And a thorough look at culture and scripture will prove that the presence of hardship is necessary, if not useful.

A Cultural And A Biblical Review Of Hardship

The culture we live in embraces the concept of hardship in many ways, from birthing, the educational process, war, athletics, farming, and even our vocations. It takes hard work to be successful at these. I'm sure everyone recognizes the value of hardship in our culture, although most of us would prefer that hardship and adversity are time controlled, come with moderation, and never happen to us.

References to hardship fill the cultural narrative in America. American commercialism, advertising, slogans, and catchphrases scream hard work. There's phrases like "No pain, no gain" and "It takes a licking and keeps on ticking." The movie industry scriptwriting encourages a good fifteen-minute ending after a ninety-minute ride of pain and loss. The concept of blue-collar workers and their contributions to America is part of the fabric of our culture in the United States. So why would hardship be something that is so foreign to our personal lives?

And much like the cultural narrative, hardship fills the biblical story in many ways. Moses, Joseph, David, Esther, Daniel, the prophets, John the Baptist, Paul, the disciples and apostles, and even Jesus, the central figure of Christianity, were all subjected to hardship. All of them experienced significant trial, sickness, and adversity while at the same time ministering to others who were healed or miraculously visited by God. While most of these men and women never escaped their own hardship, each finished his or her story with a resounding win. The faith of Christianity was born out of hardship and not ease.

We could read through the difficulties that each of these people went through and write a series about the loss, pain, and brokenness he or she experienced. But remember that we could also write a series about the gain, healing, and purpose that each experienced in his or her life in the midst of his or her pain.

Hardship seems to be the human condition since the beginning of time. Even if we are reticent to accept it, one storyline throughout history cannot be denied. The presence of hardship, suffering, and pain that is pervasive in every society, on every continent, or upon the rich or poor and paupers or kings. And because of this reality, we need a shift in our thinking, a reset. We are not to think that God will keep us from hardship, suffering, and pain. But that He will keep us in it.

Instead we should be learning to embrace difficulty, cope with it, and use it like resistance to a strength trainer, wind force to a jetliner, or the burial of a seed before it produces fruit. Walk humanity back through every century until the beginning of time, and you will see hardship, suffering, and pain as the common denominator globally and without respect to persons.

This book is a look at the presence and purpose of hardship and pain as told through the story of our family and Job, one of the central figures of the Old Testament. As you can see in the title of the book, the idea behind the writing of this book is to create a quick and easy read of a very difficult subject. Like Twitter, the writing style of the book is succinct.

If Job had Twitter in his day, what kind of an impact could he have had? I'm sure his posts on Twitter or other social-media platforms would have received many likes and retweets with the kind of life he lived and the words he could have posted. I'll have more about Job in a minute.

I will include many references to the apostle Paul and his writing in this book. This is certainly not an exhaustive study on hardship, suffering, and pain, but even a surface discussion on the matter would not be complete if Paul were not a part of the conversation. As the central figure of the New Testament, Paul was another great example of how to overcome against all odds. It's interesting that arguably some of the most prominent figures of the Bible experienced almost unbelievable hardship—Moses, Joseph,

David, the prophets, Mary, Jesus, Paul, and the apostles. And yet they have impacted Christianity as much as any persons in human history.

Throughout the Bible, there are countless references to hardship producing maturity, strength, relationship, faith, and trust. You will see many people in the Bible who exhibited great character while walking through hardship. And they almost embraced it as a part of life instead of avoiding it. This is a great revelation that, when understood, revolutionizes how we look at suffering. After all, there are as many verses addressing hardship in the Bible that ask, "How long, Lord" as there are verses that ask "Why me, Lord?"

Maybe as we are going through hardship, it would help if we would take these biblical examples as models on how we should go through adversity. The biblical record certainly proves that you are not the only one going through some kind of suffering. Hardship is not unique to you. And the cultural record is proof as well.

As we look at our story and the account of Job, we will discover nine keys that will help us navigate hardship. Each chapter is the message behind a tweet that Job would have tweeted if he had a Twitter account during his lifetime. There are words of wisdom, comfort, or correction from a man who went through a lot of difficulty. There is no doubt in my mind that Job would have had many more followers than our presidents, Justin Bieber, and the Kardashians because his life was not unlike many of us living in America.

How many people are as honest as Job with their social media? I think it would be refreshing to read real tweets instead of the highlights that most of us portray. We may not all be as wealthy or as pious as Job was. But all have experienced hardship to some degree, which places us in proximity with Job in a unique way. And what is so compelling about Job is that he went through so much more hardship than most of us will ever go through in our lifetime. And he modeled to us how to do it with purpose.

Another powerful concept used in this book is the symbol of *My Broken Palace*, the title of the Spoken Word at the beginning of the book. I wrote this after reading a pamphlet entitled *My Broken Palace*. It is a great interactive and online resource for anyone going through difficulty.

I also wrote that spoken word because of the many thousands of stories I have heard from leaders and students across America. They are the evidence that, even though things might look okay in our nation, we have a lot of problems. And at some point, we must reconcile the reality of hardship and pain with our privileged thinking and how we are going to deal with the reality of suffering. What all of us need to understand is that hardship, grace, and beauty can exist in the same place. That grace actually works best in hardship, in *My Broken Palace*.

To be honest, because of the hardship that our family has gone through the past couple of years I would not define me as an expert on suffering. That would be a disservice to many of my friends who are serving in countries without the freedom and provision that we have in America. And it would be a huge disservice to the poor and the vulnerable globally. So, this book simply contains the many lessons that our family learned over the past year or so. As you read through this book, you will learn many great lessons from the story of Job and what our family went through. And these tweets will guide you successfully as you experience hardship in your own life. I believe that each of these tweets will help you navigate the deep water and the intense heat of hardship so that, when you get to the end of your story, like Job and our family, you too will win.

Chapter 1
MY BROKEN PALACE

*God is in the slums, the cardboard boxes where the poor
play house. And He is with us, if we are with them.*

—Bono

Hardship and suffering is relative. What some believe is hardship, others
would not agree with. Much of that depends upon where we live. Or, how
we were raised. This book is not about classifying hardship and suffering.
That would be a debate far too difficult to tackle. And it would be unfair.
Because hardship and suffering are personal.

In America, we are the envy of the world, and we seem to live our lives in a
fairy-tale existence. To most of the world, we live in a big mansion with all
of the right clothes and stuff. We don't have a care in the world. And in our
own mind, we pretty much feel the same way. We feel elite and privileged,
and our expectations are mostly unrealistic.

But consider the reality that our palaces are actually broken, inhabited by
jesters and dragons, cracks and crevices, princes who go out to war, and
princesses banished in the castle who can never go out. No matter what
type of panacea we dream up, our life as American or Christian is still a
broken palace. But that's okay because things aren't perfect yet. Someday

they will be. But for now, we live in a broken world, no matter how much we want it to be otherwise. Just look at the Twittersphere and social media. While everything is being shaken around us, you can go to social media and find instant positivity and outlook that we know is not completely real. Someone has rightly said that we should not be comparing someone's social-media highlights to our everyday lowlights or "B-roll." That is simply not a fair evaluation. It's almost like most users of social media are trying to reset their lives by posting.

However, given this propensity for positivity, we can learn many things on these media platforms. Aside from the educational and inspirational take-aways, social-media platforms have made our global village into more of a "glocal" village, one that has shrunk the world into the palm of our hands.

Take Twitter, for instance. Statista, the statistics portal company, declared that Twitter has about three hundred million active users globally, as of the first quarter of 2017. According to the same company, Facebook passed a billion in 2015. That's a lot of people talking. Where else can you be connected to family, friends, or interests so quickly?

Job On Twitter
If there is one person you would want to follow on Twitter, if he had an account, it would be Job. The Bible tells the story of Job in the Old Testament. Job was a man of integrity and high character in the land of Uz, in the Palestinian desert region. He had a large family of ten children and was very wealthy and respected in the province. And he lived on a palatial property with cattle, vineyards, workers, pools, and many resources. He had a large family of ten children, and his property would rival any expensive land today.

With a life like that, you would think that Job had it easy. Living in a palace like Job with all of the stuff would certainly make life easy for him and his family, right? Try again. It wasn't smooth sailing for Job. Because of hardship, his story actually looks more like a nightmare than a dream.

What a backdrop for a platform of social influence! Job had it all and then lost it all. You can't make this stuff up. You might call his life "made for TV" or "made for social-media." Twitter is a social-media tool that has networked the globe. Initially the idea was to create a simple platform for social statements, relationship building, or presence that uses 140 characters and required inspiration and creative thought. Mostly positive and affirming, the tweets, or posts have become the daily drug of this generation.

And it has become more evolving as Twitter has gone viral. It has now become a news and educational source and advertising and marketing tool for not only individuals but every kind of organization on the planet. Prompting users to wax poetic and become wordsmiths to try to attract a following of people who like what they are posting on a regular basis. The more likes and retweets that a user has, the greater high he or she receives from the drug. And the impact of these statements is far-reaching. Imagine if there were a point to the thoughts we tweeted or read.

Enter Job into the fray. Because of the almost unbelievable hardship, suffering, and pain that he experienced in life and given his poetic wordsmith, we could all relate to Job's Twitter feed in some way. And he would be an inspirational follow for sure.

The story of Job is found in the book of Job of the Old Testament. Job was an icon, the stuff of legend. Some claim the story of Job is simply an Old Testament parable, an allegory, a myth, or the greatest story ever told. Others, including the prophets and even references in the Koran, hold the book of Job to be factual and part of biblical historicity.

If you haven't heard the story of Job, here is the short. As one of the key figures in the Old Testament, he was an interesting example of a life dedicated to God. Even though he was righteous and wealthy, hardship came down upon Job with a swift vengeance. The story opens in what is called the prologue, a scene in heaven where Satan approaches God and sets up the narrative. Satan claims that Job was so blessed on earth only because God was protecting him. So Satan wanted to unleash upon Job many trials to test his faith, proving to God and everyone else that Job wasn't really righteous. Job was only faithful to God because God had blessed him. At the end of this opening conversation, God gives permission for Satan to bring hardship into Job's life.

And with God's permission, Satan brought great loss of land, buildings, and property; death to the workers under Job's care; and natural disaster to his home. All ten of his children were killed. And with one final blow, Satan plagued Job with physical disease that wracked his body in pain.

And yet through all of the hardship that Satan brought into Job's life, Job never cursed God, sinned, or walked away from his faith in God. Watching over him this entire time, God must have been pleased with Job and his response to difficulty. Throughout the story of Job, there are visits from friends who try to help, contemplative conversations about inequity and suffering and God's nature that Job has with himself. And there are legendary conversations between Job and God.

In the end of the story, because of Job's faithfulness and character and because of his deep resolve and God's great grace, Job receives double everything he had lost during the time of hardship. Additionally, God has the final word in Job's life at the end of the book, and we do not hear any more of Satan's involvement in the story. Proving once again of the limits that Satan has on the earth and in our lives.

In each chapter of this book, we are going to look at some of the great moments of the story of Job that will become lessons for you and me. This will include how to navigate hardship, suffering, and pain and to come out better than how we came into the hardship. Another angle in the book is the use of our family story.

When Hardship Becomes Personal

Through the recent death of my wife, I've had to rethink everything I believe in. Do I believe everything I have preached and taught over four decades of ministry? Certainly, if He is God of the mountains, then He is God of the valleys. And just like Job, hardship came to us. It has no favorites. It falls on the just and the unjust. But as I have walked through the toughest year of my life, hardship began to create purpose in me.

This purpose rose out of the worst time in our life, yet it is guiding me along the way of healing and leading me to a greater spiritual maturity. And if I were not thinking right, I would have wasted the hardship that was coming my way. One thing for sure, you do not want to waste hardship, suffering, and pain. If you do, you may have to go through it again and again until you learn how to use it for your advantage.

I had a much different view of hardship when it wasn't prevalent in my life. As a pastor, I had compassion on people in hardship. Working with teens, I would cry with students who were suffering and then go home to my family. During counseling sessions, it was easy for me to feel sympathy with people who were in pain. Often my remedy for people who were going through hardship, suffering, and pain was simplistic. I would tell them to have patience, or I would tell them they were not the only one going through something. I can recall telling people to see through God's eyes and get His perspective. Often I would ask them what God was teaching them. And there were times when I would ask them to look at Paul or Job's situation and count their blessings that they are not going through what they did. And I would most every time pray with them. But is that all there is to it? Sympathy, instruction, and prayer?

Looking back at these times when I was helping others, I wish I knew then what I know now. Oh, I probably would have given some of the same advice. But I would provide it with much more compassion, brokenness, and assurance. It is much easier to settle with hardship until it becomes personal. It is much easier to admit it exists in our culture until it becomes personal. And we can even understand hardship better and counsel others from a safe place until adversity becomes personal. And once hardship becomes personal, it is almost impossible not to be intentional with our response to others when they are in a time of suffering. Experiencing hardship creates compassion and purpose in those who are willing to be trained by it.

When hardship becomes personal, something changes. The hardship of others moves us. We even feel pity or, better yet, mercy. When the news-lead talks about a tsunami in Indonesia, a mudslide in Japan, fires in the West, a tornado in the Midwest, or a hurricane in the Gulf, we are ready to give to an aid organization or to give counsel. But when it becomes personal, we are crippled. And our response is completely different. The purpose of this book is to get you to see that hardship can be a great trainer. And that our response should be with empathy and compassion.

Call it unfamiliarity, elitism, or specialness. If you can get past the thought of hardship as a curse or everyone else's problem, you will be able to accept and use hardship to your advantage and the good of others as well. After all, even though your palace might be broken, it is still a palace. There's a purpose in everything. If you are careful and intentional, you can see the same kind of purpose rise out of your situation as Job, my family, and I did in ours.

When Hardship Hits The Palace

The picture on the cover of this book says it all. We have this dichotomy in America: one of a pristine palace and another of the imperfect palace. We perceive the beautiful facade of the palace, and we see the reality of what lies within the palace. We observe what we have created with make-up, clothes, social-media, and spin. And then we see what we are actually like on the inside.

> *This dichotomy is like looking at the cover of the book, what we have created in our mind and what really exists. We simply cannot allow for any kind of imperfection into our world. Hardship is mostly an unwelcome visitor in our lives. We like the kings and queens. We like the steeples and gardens. But what do we do with the jesters and the dragons?*

Our perspective on hardship could be the key. Understanding the value of hardship is a game-changer in our lives. Face it. All of us live in a castle that is under attack in some way. Whether we live in a castle, an urban apartment, a suburban Cape Cod, a rural farmhouse, or a slum, all of us face difficulty of some type. What matters most is how we respond to it when it shows up at our address. Are we prone to complain, anger, isolation, blame, or bitterness? Or do we take responsibility and action and step back with perspective, or seek counseling? We will deal with all of these responses throughout the book. What is important to understand is that we may have to unlearn many things in order to think with the right mind. Much of what we have learned is contrary to how God views hardship.

Upside Down

I have a friend who is an artist/painter. As a communicator, he has a unique gift of using art and painting to illustrate his messages. One of the ways he communicates with his art is very interesting. As he is painting, you can barely recognize the artistry and his strokes, and what he is trying to accomplish. The colors and lines seem confusing. As a matter of fact,

I remember watching him for the first time and thinking, *This guy is not very good. I could that.*

But as the presentation progressed, I began to notice something in his work. As he came to the end of his communication art, he did something very peculiar. I'm sure that everywhere he goes people have the same response that I did, watching this distinguished and professional artist and wondering what is taking place on the canvas in front of me.

But he wasn't finished. And after many minutes of painting toward the end of his work, he simply takes the canvas and turns it upside right to reveal the masterpiece. What made no sense to our eyes was now very clearly a skillful work of art. What we have been observing in the past ten to fifteen minutes of Eric Samuel Timm's painting was that he was painting upside down. Once the canvas was turned upside right, everything was clear. As great as an artist that Eric is, the process of his illustration becomes the asset. You have to wait until the end and see from the artist's point of view.

Apply this illustration in your own life. Sometimes we cannot make sense of what God is doing. We're thinking, *How could He do this to me? Why is there so much pain and suffering in the world? I thought that God was all powerful.* We need to realize that God is the master painter. But He's not done yet. And when He is finished, He will turn everything upside right so we can actually see what He has been doing the whole time. And trust me. Just like I've seen in my own life, God will turn the mess upside right, and it will be beautiful.

While I have been studying the book of Job, it seems like the story is upside down. It's not right. Here is a young man who was righteous, a noble man in the city, and a friend of God. And yet the rest of the story seems upside down and unfair. But you cannot simply look at the beginning of the story. You have to read to the end of it, where God restores everything back to Job and shows us that He has a purpose for everything in our lives. And everything looks upside right again!

There is more to the palace story than what we see. If we see our lives as a portrait God is painting, He is not done with the picture. When an artist begins to work, we might look at the portrait or painting and think the picture is terrible. It's just lines and half thoughts on a canvas. But just like an artist's unfinished work, if things don't look right, God is not done. I believe the story of Job is similar. While reading the story of Job, we are thinking that this isn't fair. God is unjust. How could He allow this to happen to such a great person?

After we get to the end of reading about Job's life, we see how God used Job's problems for His purposes. All of a sudden, if we are faithful and persistent during hardship, our mess is turned into His message. If we are patient in suffering, we see His presence instead of our pain. When we choose to trust in God's purposes, He places our chaos on to a canvas and creates His masterpiece. And ultimately, in our hardship, suffering, and pain, our gray world becomes a blast of colors in the end.

The importance of going to the end cannot be overstated. Be careful of getting caught in the moment and missing the opportunity of a lifetime as you go through difficulty. Someday you will talk with someone who actually lived through crisis.

Conversations At Cafeteria Tables
Can you imagine at the end of your life, experiencing the mercy that allows us to heaven, having the opportunity to speak with the saints of the scriptures and all of the Christians who have gone before us? In our presence for eternity will be the martyrs who built the church before us, the Christians who were tortured during the crusades, the apostles and disciples who walked with Christ and wrote the scriptures we have today, the prophets from the centuries before Christ whose words are chronicled in

the Old Testament, and the angels who have visited humanity since the beginning of time. Of great importance and interest to me will be my conversations with Job and the apostle Paul.

Allow me to stretch your imagination for a minute. One afternoon in heaven, you walk into the cafeteria and notice an empty seat over at Job and Paul's table. It's your chance to speak with two of the most iconic figures in the Bible, two of the central figures of Christianity. As you approach the table with your tray, Job motions with his hand for you to be seated. Nervously you sit and are at a loss for words.

And Paul simply says to you, "Shalom. What's your story?"

Now, I'm not sure how they will speak in heaven or what language will be used, so stay with me. What will be your response? Remember who you are seated next to.

I think most of us will respond with something like this, "Well, guys, see, I, uh, I'm from America. The United States. And it was rough. I don't know about you guys, but I mean, my school was tough on me. I went to See You At The Pole one year, and they mocked me all day. I had to stop bringing my Bible because they were so rude and condescending. Calling me names and stuff. And there were times when I thought, *God, where are you?* You know what I mean?"

As Paul and Job turn and look at each other with a blank stare on their faces and then pick up their trays and walk away, do you realize what you just said? To Paul and Job? Let me remind you of their suffering, hardship, loss, pain, and disappointment in life. They were in peril from family and friends, dangers at sea, sickness to their bodies, beatings from a mob, and imprisonment for the gospel. Let me remind you that each was within hours of his life. And they lost their integrity before all of their family and friends for the sake of God.

Both Paul and Job lost everything. And you want to talk about friends who mocked you for going to See You At The Pole, coworkers who isolated you in the office, or peers who were rude because you prayed for your meal at lunch, or strangers who laughed at you because you are Christian?

There is always more to the story. Think about the palace where Job lived and all of the things he possessed. Sometimes we get fixated on the losses, don't we? And we forget there is so much to gain in every story. Or look at the picture in your mind of a castle on acres of land in the middle of a meadow. It is picturesque and the stuff of folklore, like the scenes throughout *The Sound of Music.*

While looking at Job's story, it can be easy to see the dross or the loss and the malice in the palace. Too often we get focused on the wrong thing. Do we see that God is in the slums where the poor play humbly? And do we see that God is in the castle where the rich play proudly? And do you know that God is with us if we are with them? Don't give up on yourself, your situation, or God. If things are really bad right now, it is not over. If Job Had Twitter, he would tell you the same thing. No matter how broken the palace is, it is still a palace. When you get to the end of the story, Job wins. And when you get to the end of your story, you can win. We did.

Getting to the end of the story requires a fight, effort, or battle. We all have to learn this. That it is worth fighting till the end. Maybe you have seen the poster with a cat hanging onto a rope that is many feet off the ground. Clinging to the rope with one paw, the quote on the poster says, "Even if you only have one paw on the rope, never let go."

I was talking with a young teen in Idaho one afternoon, and she taught me this valuable lesson of waiting and not giving up, of fighting and learning to conquer whatever is in your way. We should finish the story all the way to the end. If we are breathing, we still have a chance. The lesson she taught me was that, "If things are bad, it is not the end. In the end, things are never bad. God always works them out for good. God always wins in the end."

I mean, we all have said that, and we probably even believe that. At least until we are in the story and experiencing the hardship or suffering.

Somehow, coming from a teenager, it carries more weight. Especially from this young girl in Idaho who would never quit. These words were so much more meaningful because of her situation. She said this to me from her wheelchair.

#ifjobhadtwitter Every palace has jesters and dragons, and princes and princesses, who grow up to be kings and queens, who slay dragons

Chapter 2
A BASTARD'S REWARD

*God did have a Son on earth without sin. But He
did not have a Son on earth without suffering.*

—Augustine

A bastard's reward is ease and comfort. Why? Bastards have no one to care for them, father them, and discipline and train them. They are on their own and without ceilings and fences free to run and play. Now I am not using *ease* and *comfort* as a good thing, unless only in the bastard's mind. For ease and comfort are not the way to a good life and certainly not the way to a productive and mature existence. It takes a father or a parent or a mentor to help create that. And no good parent would ever allow for his or her children to be raised in complete ease and comfort. And so a bastard's reward is a life without parenting, discipline, and training.

Right away you might be thinking, *That's the problem I have with Christianity.* Or you may be pondering, *Why would I want to be adopted into the family of discipline or suffering?* All of us have said or thought, "If God were so good, why is there evil? How can evil and God exist together?"

There really is an easy answer to those questions. The answer is another question: which family do you want to go through hardship and suffering with? No doubt you are going through or have gone through hardship in the past year. Then why not go through it with the right people? And why not go through hardship for the right purpose? Make no mistake about it. You will be adopted into a family when it comes to hardship, suffering, and pain. Which family you are adopted into depends upon your response to hardship. Try to avoid it, and you become a bastard. Be trained by it, and you become a son.

If you are human, you will go through hardship. If you are without faith when you go through hardship, you are adopted into the family of grief, the family of anger, the family of blame, or, the family of bitterness. But if you are luckier, you are adopted into the family of Alcoholics Anonymous or the family of professional clinical counseling.

However, the best adoption when you are going through hardship is with the family of God and redeeming what you are experiencing with a higher purpose, with people who will love you and help you through hardship. You need to know that you are choosing the family that you will go through life with every day.

Hebrews 12

Over the past year in our family, we have been learning many lessons about hardship. Nobody is immune from trials. Nor should we desire to be immune from trials. Let me prove that by taking you to scripture. I have been reading through Hebrews 12 as preparation for this book. After reading through this chapter, a statement Paul makes is a game-changer when it comes to hardship. He begins this passage of scripture with a challenge for our lives. "Endure hardship like a son..."

Listen to the rest of the words from Paul as he defines the concept of hardship, discipline, and family,

> My son, do not make light of the Lord's discipline, and do not lose heart when he rebukes you, because the Lord disciplines the one

he loves, and he chastens everyone he accepts as his son. Endure hardship as discipline; God is treating you as his children. For what children are not disciplined by their father? If you are not disciplined—and everyone undergoes discipline—then you are not legitimate, not true sons and daughters at all...No discipline seems pleasant at the time, but painful. Later on, however, it produces a harvest of righteousness and peace for those who have been trained by it (Hebrews 12.5–8, 11).

Athletes know this principle of "No pain, no gain." Crops reap the benefit of this principle of "No rain, no gain." Paul said it well in Hebrews 12 when he said that, if we are not going through hardship, we are not His sons. We are illegitimate. The word is *bastard*. Paul was saying that if we don't receive discipline and chastening we are not legitimate. But if we do receive discipline and chastening we are children with a parent.

The argument and ultimately the answer to suffering is all about character and nature, and not only the character and nature of you and me. But God's! Here it is. God is kind because it is His nature to be kind. And He is good because goodness is His character. He will often use His kindness and goodness to bring a little tough love our way. Paul said we should "endure hardship because then God is dealing with us as sons. And if you do not partake in hardship, you are illegitimate" (Heb. 12.7–9). The parental nature of God includes all means to raise His children. Sometimes that might be hardship.

God has a weird way of loving us sometimes, doesn't He? I mean, using hardship to discipline me or allowing it into my life to mature me isn't one of my love languages! But it is one of God's. Now that is a thought.

Gary Chapman made this teaching a hit back in the early 1990s with his book, *The Five Love Languages*, defining the way that people were to love their spouse. They included gifts, quality time, words of affirmation, acts of service, and physical touch. You might say that God has shown His love for His bride in all of these ways, for instance, when He bestowed the spiritual gifts upon us (1 Cor. 12; Rom. 10).

Or there were so many times Jesus pulled away from everything going around them just to be alone with the disciples for quality time (Mark 13.13–19). What about how He used words of affirmation to the children playing near Him and the disciples, the woman caught in adultery, the demoniac from Gadara, the disciples after His resurrection, Peter after his denial, and other people in distress (Matt. 19; Mark 5; Luke 24.46–49; John 21.15–19). Jesus even stated that the reason He came to the earth was to give and to serve with legendary acts of service (Matt. 20.28). And while everyone was trying to stop her from getting to Him, Jesus allowed the woman with the blood problem to touch Him. Physical touch was certainly fulfilled in Jesus's ministry to His generation as He laid hands on the people countless times, the disciples rested on Him, and He lived among the people incarnate (Mark 5).

But hardship isn't one of Chapman's love languages. It is, however, one of the ways God loves us.

The Concept Of Family
God defined His love through the family. Jesus was deeply committed to the family institution by setting an example and a culture of family in almost everything He did. Remember His words on the cross to John? He introduced Mary and John and asked them to be a surrogate family and to model to everyone around them how family takes care of each other in difficulty. Of course, the main reason He did this was knowing that John would really need family once Jesus was gone. Jesus even extended the concept of family to those who were not His immediate family. Remember when He told the crowds not to worry about Him being home with His family? He felt He was with family when He was with them (Mark 3). Or what about the people He healed and told to go and show their family?

And Jesus loved to eat with the people and build a concept of family when He was in their home for dinner. There is no denying that family was very important to God throughout the scriptures. This is why it is so important to choose the right family in the midst of hardship and to place ourselves under the care of the family of God.

Hardship is prevalent in this generation in many forms. And it can be seen also in the breakup and disintegration of the family. And this adds to the problem of healing. Broken homes, the redefinition of marriage, drug/alcohol abuse, self-harm, sexual revolution, social-media distraction, and an identity crisis have added to the breakdown of a generation. In my work with young people, I have never seen the disintegration of the family like today. Encouraging stats show drug and alcohol abuse is going down but its use is increasing. Never have I seen so much depression in my work with young people. One stat says there are thirty million people in America who are clinically depressed. And the sexual revolution has crushed the biblical identity of teens who are being fed the deception of a neutral-gender personage.

If anyone can relate to this generation of young people and their condition, Christ can. He went through everything that we have gone through. And when we know Him, we are able to use our hardship and suffering to influence others who are going through it. We are in the fellowship or family of God. Of suffering, Paul said in Philippians 3.10, "That I may know Him, His death, His resurrection, and His suffering." It's probably not the prayer we often pray for ourselves. But it is a powerful prayer that can help us to prepare for injustice or inequity. God's Son modeled both blessing and suffering.

A Jungle Or A Garden?
The American dream is no longer a garden. It has been overrun with weeds and unwanted pests. And it looks more like a jungle. The American dream castle that our young people think they are living in is really cracked at its foundation. And it looks more like a dungeon.

But there is hope. The brokenness of this generation is real. Today, because teen lives and the teen world are so messed up, young people try to put on pretty, peace, and value. They try to dress up their brokenness. But you cannot put paint over rust, Band-Aids over a broken arm, or even a dress on a pig. Because they will still be rusted, broke, and ugly. I have received hundreds of letters, emails, and personal conversations from students about the kind of broken things they are dealing with today—broken homes, broken relationships, broken dreams, broken promises, broken bodies, and broken hearts.

> *The palace that we have called the American dream has become a nightmare. It is simply broken. Fallen-ness has infested the castle. But lying inside of every palace is a king and a queen.*

Look at these texts and their definition of the home and the spiritual and physical structure of the family. In Amos 9.11, it says, "In that day I will restore David's fallen tent. I will repair its broken places, restore its ruins, and build it as it used to be." Proverbs 24.30–31 reads, "I went past the field of the lazy man, past the vineyard of the man who lacks judgement...and its wall was broken down." And Proverbs 25.28 states, "Like a city whose walls are broken down is a man who lacks self-control." Each of these describe the importance of the home, the discipline, and the preparation it takes to maintain and repair the home, proving the place of the Bible in the answer to the problem of pain. A healthy home!

When Princes And Princesses Become Kings And Queens

It is not our responsibility to raise princes and princesses. It is our responsibility to raise kings and queens. Inside every prince is a king. And inside every princess is a queen. And it is our responsibility to pull it out of them. Our prayer is that what we are going through as a family will model to this generation the purpose of God upon our lives and the faithfulness of God to those who serve Him. And it is to show this generation that God will redeem every moment of our lives. It is our responsibility to tell the story. As the apostle John said in the New Testament letter in 3 John 1.4, "I have no greater joy than to hear that my children walk in truth."

One of the greatest joys in this whole crisis for our family is to see my kids' response to their mother's death and to see their strength and honesty in all of this. Through their response to our hardship and suffering, I have watched my two boys become kings and my daughter become a queen in the crucible of suffering.

The other great joy of my life is watching the young people around me rising up and responding with such great spirituality and service. In the midst of my suffering, I have been impacted by so many young people personally through texts and messages, by email, and on my social media platforms. The family of Christianity in the church is unique. When tested by hardship, the family gets stronger and comes to the aid of the weaker. The truth is, watching the young people who have been in my life over the past year has been humbling. Many times, as I would arrive to an event or venue, teenagers I do not even know would be there would provide words of encouragement, telling me they have been praying for me. And I hear them say to me that they have been impacted by our story so much that it has helped them overcome in their situation. To see what we have gone through by helping teenagers wade through the waters of life and come out on the other end better and not bitter has been a great reward to me.

During the last year or so, my message to this generation has been simple:

1. See the brokenness in the palace. Don't be afraid to admit the problem. The facade can sometimes hide reality. Hidden in the secret place beyond the makeup and the labels is a broken young man and lady. Look deeper at the palace and love it. Sure, it may look like a garden on the outside, but if you look closely, there is a

jungle in the life of every teenager. Admitting that will be the first step to dealing with it.

2. Allow the brokenness to shape you into a king or queen. Don't let it cripple you or keep you from ultimate royalty. There is nothing like hardship, suffering, and pain to create maturity and discipline in our lives. It is the road to kingship and queenship for each of us. You might call it the road less travelled, something that ease cannot create. Do not take lightly the impact of the School of Hard Knocks and the University of Suffering as a trainer for our spiritual development.

3. See the beauty of the palace. There are hurts, rebellion, lies, fear, and materialism. But residing alongside of these things is also something very beautiful. Do you see the healing, obedience, truthfulness, courage, grace, and sacrifice? All of us have observed the real message in pop culture and the hardship in the music, movies, peers, language, and narrative of twenty-first-century America. But alongside the hardship, present in the pain, is another message. The message of the Father to His children.

We also see in culture and scripture that the message of the Church is set in every community, a ready presence in the middle of hardship and difficulty. And the message of the church is family, hope, redemption, and grace. That's right. Present alongside the brokenness is the beauty. The idea behind *My Broken Palace* is simple. We often picture our lives as pristine castles and portray our lives as ornate palaces without corruption or blemish when, in reality, we are really broken.

I see it all the time in America. A machismo says, "I'm okay; you're okay." Pop psychology cannot deal with the reality of suffering. The impact of this book is that, in the end, every story of brokenness finishes with beauty. Every account turns into a brag session on how God redeems difficulty.

The Family In Suffering

Our family has seen healing. We've seen God heal my son Justen in our kitchen of painful and obvious warts on his hand in just days. After months of treatment by doctors, Justen was frustrated with the warts on his hand. As a football player, they would be painful from being broken open, and he would have to bandage them often just to hide them. They really became an embarrassment to him. While finishing up dinner one evening, Justen was upset.

Jane became frustrated as well and called all of us to pray. I've learned that when Jane gets upset that we need to listen to her. So I went to the cupboard and got the olive oil that we used often as a symbol of the Holy Spirit when we prayed for the family. As I poured oil on his hand, we prayed together as a family. There was no emotional moment or feeling of faith. I felt that I was being just as obedient to Jane as I was the Holy Spirit. To be honest, we had done this many times. But this would be the last time we needed to pray for Justen. After we prayed that night, Justen's warts were gone in days and never came back!

And I'll never forget in the middle of the night when we heard the Lord walk into our home and heal our oldest son Jaren instantly after he was coughing for days and lying in bed one evening. We tried medicine, water, and prayer. But he stayed home from school and continued to cough uncontrollably and lost his voice over a couple of days.

In frustration, I just simply said, "God, I can't handle this anymore."

As we lay in bed frustrated, Jane and I heard steps in the hallway and thought one of the kids had gotten up to go to the bathroom or something. I didn't hear any toilet flush or see a light come on so I got up to check on the kids. While I was doing that I noticed that Jaren had stopped coughing. I went into his room and he was sound asleep. When I walked back into our bedroom, we knew in that moment as we looked at each other in the middle of the night that God had come into our home and healed Jaren.

Another healing that took place in our family happened when our daughter Jorie was facing a difficult surgery of a tumor in her neck that was perilously close to the nerves in her face and neck. The doctors told us that the place of the tumor could cause her to become paralyzed, and a risky surgery would take four to six hours.

We left Jorie and went to the family waiting room. But just ninety minutes later, the doctors came out walking down the hall and into the waiting room. I must admit in that moment that I was not full of faith. My first thought was that something had gone wrong. But the doctor told us, "The surgery was remarkable. The tumor almost fell out of her neck when we opened her up. That doesn't happen to hardened tumors." Once again, our family had seen God step into our lives and change the story.

In the same way, in the middle of Job's story of hardship and pain, losing even his children and having a wife that was buried under the stress, Job brings us some of the great moments of tragedy and suffering in history. His response to hardship is legendary. And in the end, his family is restored to him. After going through unprecedented depression and physical circumstances of sickness, the final chapters of Job's story are somewhat matter-of-fact, a stunning reward for the dignity he displayed in the face of historic suffering. We see Job partying with his family after God blessed him with double the resources he had before the tragedy.

I love the emphasis in the old hymns of the Church on our Father's presence in our hardship. An old hymn we used to sing said it this way, "Some through the waters, some through the flood. Some through the fire, but all through the blood. Some through great sorrow, but God gives a song, In the night season and all the day long." The presence of a heavenly Father in suffering makes all the difference.

A God Who Is Wet And On Fire

God is totally concerned with your situation. That is why He is in it with you. Stop worrying and looking at the water and the fire. God said, "When you pass *through* the waters, I will be with you. And *through* the rivers, they will not sweep over you. And when you walk *through* the fire, you will not be burned" (Isaiah 43.2).

Most of us think that God cannot swim and He is going to melt under the intense heat of life. But we serve a God who is wet, in the deep, and on fire. Even so, the water hasn't drowned Him. The flood hasn't washed Him away, and the fire doesn't burn Him. Understand that I am not trying to minimize your problem. What I am trying to do is maximize your God.

I hear stories every week of how life is breaking down teenagers. But God cannot be someone He is not. And He is with you in it. He is an ever-present help in time of need (Psalm 46.1). If you look at the teen culture, you will see that everything is falling around them. So many of the systems around teenagers are falling apart—their family and peers, the entertainment industry, and even the American culture. With all of the shaking going on around teenagers, the church must remain stable and present. And it is the role of the church to build healthy families.

Paul said in the letter to the Corinthians, "If any man be in Christ, he is a new creation, the old things have passed away, and behold, all things are made new" (2 Cor. 5.17).

Do you see the emphasis there? If anyone be in Christ, in the body of Christ and in the family of God, there is health and wholeness. One thing I have learned in this season of our lives is that our soul poverty is God's sole priority. And it is the role of the church to build healthy families. The church should be operating with the soul as its priority. The word "in" is a very important word in Paul's text. Do not forsake assembling together in church with the family of God. We need a renewed involvement in the church. It must become a priority for believers.

> *One of the most important moments of Jesus's life was when He was lost from His family as a preteen. After looking for Him for days, they found Him in the youth group. Well, actually they found Him in the temple. That's a great thought. The only scripture we have of Jesus as a teen (pre-teen actually) is of Him in the youth group! If you get lost, make sure you are lost in church and not the world.*

Job was able to deal with this situation because he was righteous and a man of character. But underlying the entire story is the presence of God as the head of Job's home. God doesn't leave us when things get tough. As a matter of fact, he does his greatest work in the midst of our greatest need. God is not intimidated by darkness. The underlying reality of the story is that, when we look at Job's life, we see how important it is to stay close to God, the head of the family, even though Job's family was missing.

My daughter Jorie taught me one of the lessons I learned from our family. We were talking about the problem of pain and suffering one day and how we all face disease, sickness, accidents, and sometimes even satanic opposition. She shared with me the verse in Romans 16.10, "The God of peace will soon crush Satan under your feet." And in Romans 16.20, it reads, "And the peace of God, which transcends all understanding, will guard your hearts and your minds in Christ Jesus." Paul wrote this, which makes it even more powerful.

After quoting this verse to me, Jorie said, "Hearing this from Paul means everything. A man who experienced such legendary personal pain and loss. If Paul can make it through what he experienced in life, then we certainly can. Dad, it [the scripture] says soon. That means we have to fight. We have to overcome things. But God will always bring peace, and He always wins. Keep going even when it's hard because the end will soon be victorious!"

God Cannot Be Someone He Is Not

This can be easier said than done. But at the end of the difficulties in our family, here's what I have learned about hardship. People have told you that, if God were fair, kind, and concerned about you, why did this happen? People have said that God is not near you. You may think that God is unfair, unkind, and unconcerned with you and your situation. People look at Job as the poster child for oppression, tragedy, and suffering. And God left Him. And you are the poster child for an unfair God. But the scriptures have proven time and again that God is attracted to hardship. God is not intimidated by hardship and suffering. It is His playing field. He just plays by different rules than we do.

Let me tell you something. God is fair because it is His nature to be. Jesus was talking about love when He said it will "rain on the just and the unjust" (Matt. 5.43–48). God is kind because it is His nature to be. And He will often use His kindness to bring a little tough love our way. Remember, Paul said we should "endure hardship because then God is dealing with us as sons. And if you do not partake in hardship, you are illegitimate" (Hebrews 12.7–9).

And God is totally concerned with your situation because it is in His nature to be. That is why He is in it with you. God said, "When you pass through the waters, I will be with you. And through the rivers, they will not sweep over you. And when you walk through the fire, you will not be burned" (Isaiah 43.2). That doesn't sound like an unfair God.

God cannot be someone He is not. Joseph said that everyone and everything that was against him and causing him harm and pain was going to work out for good. "What you have intended for evil, God has intended for good to accomplish what is now being done, the saving of many lives"

(Gen. 50.20). Remember who Joseph said this to, his family who had tried to kill him and then sell and disown him. But in the end of Joseph's story of pain, his family was standing in front of him, rejoicing that everything worked out.

No matter what your story looks like, there is one constant in the narrative. Hardship is a reality for each of us. But so is family, and so is a good and just God.

The language of this generation is hardship. They may not use it very often, but they experience it all the time. I was speaking to a group of young people after a youth service one night, and the subject turned to suffering. Each of them understood exactly what we were talking about. Suffering isn't foreign to teenagers. Each rehearsed his or her story of difficulty. For one, it was his broken family. For another, his peers and teammates were destroying his life. One girl talked about how she was bullied. And another girl cried as she talked about being raped when she was young.

As I prayed with them, I couldn't help but be broken. When we were done praying, one of the young men asked me, "Why do you do this at your age?" Now, I hear that all the time. But it felt like a compliment at the time. I just replied, "Because God told me to do this a long time ago. And He told me that, if He changed His mind, He would let me know. We talk all the time. Me and God. And He hasn't said to do anything else."

They all took me so seriously. Then one of the young ladies said, "I'm glad because you're like the dad I never had." I know I cannot be a surrogate for this generation. They really need the paternal and maternal relationship to be right. But I truly believe that, if I can model it to them, it may give them the strength to build their own home the right way.

#ifjobhadtwitter If you are going thru hardship, you are a son or daughter. If you are not going thru it, you are a bastard without a parent.

Chapter 3
WHEN GOD PLAYS CHESS

*Hey Jude, don't be afraid, take a sad song, and
make it better, remember to let her into your
heart, then you will start to make it better.*

—Paul McCartney, lyrics to "Hey Jude"

The ballad actually evolved from "Hey, Jules," a song McCartney wrote in 1968 to comfort John Lennon's son, Julian, during his parents' divorce. He told Julian, "We all live in pain. And the more pain we live in, the more we seek God."

Remember that line. "The more pain we live in, the more we seek God. The more pain we live in, the more we seek God." That was not a typo in the book. I wanted you to read that a few times. Wow! The idea behind Lennon's song is to let God in and you will start to feel better.

At the forefront of winning against hardship is trust in the designer. When God said He will have nothing before Him, He meant nothing— not your job, friends, family, and yourself. God's plan is better than ours is. If we place anything before Him, we lose His perspective. Our thinking, our family, our job, our hobbies, or even our own wisdom and ways cannot replace heaven's. The advice of The Beatles is simple yet true. In our hardship, if we place anything before God, we frustrate ourselves with replacement help, ultimately losing the perspective and possibility of what hardship and suffering are to bring into our life because we choose to. I believe we can find no relief in trying to run from pain. For it will always be there. Pain is faster than we can run, pain is louder than our silence, and pain will be running through our mind even if we close our eyes. We find our relief when we come to realize why we are going through it. We find our relief when we come to realize how long we must go through it. Our idolatry can easily make us settle for less when we are going through difficulty. However, when we place God central in our life, we then allow Him to redeem hardship and suffering for His purpose.

As the Beatles penned some other famous words in 1970, it has almost become a prophetic prose for our culture today. With the rise of hardship and suffering in our world, the words from Paul and Solomon, as well as the Beatles, are great words of comfort. The Beatles wrote,

When I find myself in times of trouble, Mother Mary comes to me
Speaking words of wisdom, let it be
And in my hour of darkness she is standing right in front of me
Speaking words of wisdom, let it be
Let it be, let it be, let it be, let it be
Whisper words of wisdom, let it be
And when the broken-hearted people living in the world agree
There will be an answer, let it be.

And thousands of years before the Beatles wrote "Let it be", Solomon wrote in Ecclesiastes 3.3–6,

A time to kill, a time to heal;
a time to break down, and a time to build up.
A time to weep, and a time to laugh;
a time to mourn, and a time to dance.

A time to gain, and a time to lose;
a time to keep, and a time to throw away.'

The palace that each of us lives in has both beauty and beast, more and least, jokers and dragons, and steeples and gardens. And in the same palace lives the landlord, God Himself. And He wants nothing more than all of us. God doesn't have an address. He has a home. That home is your palace. I guess, if He did have an address, it would be 100 Your Street, Your Town, USA And no matter what you are going through, God is present in it with you. He is with us at our address 100 percent.

God Plays Chess While We Play Checkers

From the outside, you would look at our family and think that everything was great. And yet I think many people will relate to us and the lessons we have learned over the past two years. Through a dangerous flood in our home that blew out the window above our bed while we were sleeping; a tumor and subsequent complicated surgery on our daughter's neck; our youngest son's broken back while playing football, two surgeries, and being unable to play sports; and then my wife's battle with cancer and ultimately her death, hardship became personal. As confident as I was in my spiritual life, I'm not sure anyone is prepared for what we were about to go through.

From the inside, God must have saw a few things that He wanted to deal with. And so He began to work in our lives pre-event with a precision of a strategic planner. While reading this chapter, please understand that God may be doing the same thing in your life right now. The things you are about to go through will require that you listen and observe what is occurring in your life. Maybe God is speaking to you, moving pieces, or setting up the narrative. Is God preparing you for the journey you are about to take? Since we could not model our journey live to you, will you let our family into your reading? How do you and I get to the end of our story and win? How can we assure ourselves of a great ending like Job's?

God and His ways are like a chess match, while our ways are like playing checkers. He is always working from a different, strategic perspective and a more thoughtful angle because He loves us. See, chess requires much more forethought and planning than checkers does. So many moving pieces and options are on the board when you play chess. The strategy is much more different from checkers. Proverbs 14 says that the way of a man is death. Then could the opposite be true also? That the way of God is life.

Let me explain how God was playing chess in our situation. Two things happened in the weeks before Jane's diagnosis:

1. I was prompted to read through Job and study his life. I began to create a hashtag series on my social media before I was about to go through the darkest time in my life. These tweets and words of wisdom from the book of Job were setting me up to win. Romans 8.14 says, "The sons of God are led by the Spirit of God." I am so glad that the Holy Spirit decided to walk into our situation and lead us into disciplines and patterns that would make all the difference in our life. Reading Job was just the beginning.

2. The second thing that happened just weeks before Jane's diagnosis was elementary to our success in walking through this time in our life. I was awakened in the middle of the night and challenged by God to place nothing before Him. Not even my family. When God plays chess, He is preparing us ahead of time. And because of what our family was about to go through with Jane's situation, God began to speak clearly to me and shared a warning with me that I would then share with my family and other young spiritual leaders that I was mentoring at the time.

This is how God was playing chess in our lives.

Why Does God Wake Us In The Morning All The Time?

Don't you wish that we listened to God better during the day? Then He wouldn't have to wake us in the middle of the morning! The Holy Spirit woke me on Monday, August 11, 2014, at 3:40 a.m., and gave me several warnings. I wish I had been listening clearly to Him at 3:40 p.m. at that time so He didn't have to wake me at 3:40 a.m. But He did. And I am grateful. Jane was still sleeping when the Spirit stirred me. As I lay in bed for the first few minutes, I began crying and needed to get up and leave the bedroom so I didn't wake Jane. I went into the family room and laid on the floor. And I listened.

I have not changed the words or the phrases of this awakening. It was tempting to do that to give it some current language and make it sound more graceful or palatable with prose and glamour. This is as clearly as the Lord has ever spoken to me, and I have left it as realistic as I remember. As I had been comfortably serving the Lord in my good spiritual condition, the Lord became very direct and emphatic with me. This is the question He asked me at 3:40 a.m. on Monday, August 11: "Why have I become your second thought (love)? Have I become that small in your life?"

He then asked me several more questions around two themes: familial pride and worry.

Familial Pride

The first theme was pride. And His questions were direct. "Do you know that the first two of My Ten Commandments have something to do with pride? The first is that you shall have no other God's before Me. The second is that you are not to create any image in place of me. Am I your first thought (love) or your second?"

He then asked me if I knew the other eight commandments. Thankfully I could recite each of them. This night, I would get a dose of the top ten. God checked me and my love for Him. Things were getting in the way, like family, ministry, and my reputation. So He asked me for several minutes about my pride in anything other than Him, whether that included myself, materialism, knowledge, wisdom, or my gifts and talents. He challenged me with my love for position, title, and even my master's degree. And finally, God asked me about my family, a prodding question that insinuated I had placed Jane and the kids before Him. If these were first, then He was second.

I was laying on the floor of our basement weeping. I was confused in His presence and broken from the questions. Initially when God asked me about placing my ministry and other things before Him, I was defensive. But I completely understood. There can be a lot of pride in events, things owned, talents, titles, and other things like these. And so He began to reveal my spiritual pride that was replacing Him in my life. It was natural to give up each of these things. I had placed more value in stuff that was simply worthless to Him. All of our lives, we are told that nothing should come before God, and like most everyone, I had done this prioritizing before. Now that night, just two weeks before Jane's diagnosis, I was placing God back where He belonged, as central and on the throne of my life. Right?

I was not prepared for the way He pressed me for something else, my familial pride. But as I lay there before Him early in the morning, I defended my love for my family. We needed to address situations going on in our family. When I look back, I feel that Satan had asked God for permission to work against us. Things nobody knew were happening to us. There were decisions being made, attacks against character, a flood, a serious tumor, and a broken back all signs we needed to humble ourselves and place God as preeminent in our lives again as a family.

As I lay there on the floor that night, I gave God reasons why what we were going through wasn't fair or just. And the whole time we were talking, I wasn't getting it because I was playing checkers. My logic and way of thinking was getting in the way. And that night I was learning that defending yourself against God is playing checkers to a loving Father who is playing chess.

I couldn't see past our conversation. I couldn't see the big picture. I mean, certainly God wants me to place my family as a priority in my life, right? What could be more noble than family? The problem He had was that I had placed my family as the priority in my life.

There is a difference. I needed a priority change in the most important time of my life. If there is one thing that is clear throughout scripture, it is that God is preeminent. And many of the problems that we go through in life are borne out of a place where God is not preeminent. It really is simple. Idolatry is subtle. Idolatry reorganizes our life in dangerous ways, setting us up for self-sufficiency or another kind of sufficiency that is not upon God. Everything was about to come crashing down in our lives because of this. God had to strip me of familial pride, and how He did this was abrupt. God was shaking our world of anything that would not stand. As all of these things came to a head and God was asking me to lay my family before Him, I remember thinking, *This isn't fair. Family has always been our priority.* To place family as *A* priority is noble and right. But to place family as *The* priority is not nobility. It was idolatry.

All of these other things seemed easy to let go of. But when God asked me to let go of my family, I couldn't do that. It just didn't seem right to me. You hear that? It didn't seem right to me. And that was the problem I was faced with. Listen to God or listen to me. Why would God be asking me to lay my family down just days before the greatest trial of our lives? Why wouldn't He be supporting my love for Jane and the kids just days before the battle of our lives would come? Why was He not calling us to great love and unity and relying upon each other for strength in what was about to be the toughest thing we would ever go through? If there were ever a time to rally around family, wouldn't it be now, God? God was challenging more than my idolatry. He was challenging my thinking.

It was difficult to take at first. We normally would think that a love of family is noble and a priority. But God warned me that He would not have even my family before Him. And I should quickly replace Him as the priority of my life. I remember the jealousy I felt from the Lord. It was not anger. It was like God was wanting me. His jealousy was really not even about all of the other stuff or my family. His jealousy was about Him wanting me. Instead of prioritizing everything in my life with a one through ten, what I should be doing is placing God at the center of my life.

Everything else revolves around him. Like a bicycle tire, each spoke is very important to the structure of the tire. But the most important part of the tire is the hub. The hub is the integrity of the whole structure. And God is the hub. I needed to stop numbering my life from one to ten and place God at the center of all of it. Everything else will be fine if God is at the center of the stuff.

Waking Jane
As I lay there on the floor, I knew what God was asking for, to reorganize my life and make sure the stuff was not central. That seemed like the easiest thing to do. But I also knew that God wanted me to speak to Jane and the kids about all of this. This was not going to be easy. Maybe the hardest thing I had to do was next, to wake Jane.

I began first by walking back into my bedroom around four thirty in the morning and waking Jane. I thought to myself, *If I'm going to wake her, this better be good.*

I gently nudged her and then again. When she didn't move after a couple of weak nudges, I thought that this could wait; I would just speak with her in the morning around breakfast, you know, something easier. But I knew I had to risk waking her at four thirty in the morning or trying to speak with her the next day and risk forgetting the urgency of God in that moment.

So with more intention, I woke her and began telling her what had just happened. We had the kind of relationship that valued these discussions even early in the morning so it was an easy moment for us. Actually it would have been nice if God had awakened both of us so we could hear it directly from Him. But I did my best to explain it all as she listened and responded gently throughout the whole conversation. It was like she already knew everything.

As we talked, she agreed with everything I said and even stated that God had been speaking the same thing to her for a while. And she added her thoughts. If you knew Jane, that would be no surprise that He was talking to her first. She wasn't as busy or distracted as I was. We wept and prayed together.

The next day, we contacted the kids and had them come over to the home for supper. After sharing the same thing God had spoken to me that morning, we all gave each other up and centered our lives in Christ. It was a moment for all of us. Maybe it was more ominous than any of us thought at the time. Looking back now, I see now why God plays chess while we are playing checkers. He is always several steps ahead of us.

Aside from pride, the second thing the Lord spoke to me was about worry.

Worry
This is not something I deal with. I'm not a worrier. . And these questions were direct also. "Do you trust me? Do you think that I can handle anything in your life? If you worry about anything, it is proof that you are placing it before me. Do not let worry be your first thought (love)."

I heard the Lord speaking to me about trusting Him. He was dealing with the very core of my and my family's relationship with Him. I now see why He woke me and began to prepare me for the next season of our lives. Why He woke me to prepare my family for what was about to take place.

Aside from asking about placing my family before Him, God began to deal with my trust and ultimately my worry. This was deeply convicting to me. And it became the emphasis and the strength of my life as we were about to go through the greatest trial of our lives. Again, just two weeks after this morning awakening, Jane would be diagnosed with stage four cancer out of nowhere. We had no idea that she was sick.

Why would God question us about this? I cannot even tell you anything that I was overly worried about at this time. But, God saw something be cause He was playing chess. Are you able to answer this question? What are you placing before Him? What are you worried about? Whatever it is, you must stop. It isn't worth it because He is to be our center. And He can handle anything you are going through. Trust me. Trust Him.

I realize much of an encounter with God is personal. And I have applied this to me and mine first. However, I really believe this was prophetic in nature and scope also. And I needed to direct this to the young spiritual leaders in my life as well, and so I took it to several of them. And now it becomes the theme of this chapter for you. Please don't dismiss any of this. Listen. And if there is even a small amount of something that relates to you that I have shared, please deal with it. And obey. Each of you may need to answer these questions so you could be prepared for whatever you are about to face, even if it is not a trial like ours. Deal with your pride and your worry. Even the smallest hint of defense that we might feel against this prophetic word should be the first sign that you are dealing with this in some form.

Everyone is looking for ways to deal with hardship. When we began this season in our lives, Jane began to read through Isaiah 43. The book of

Isaiah is in the Old Testament and written by one of the prophets. One of the key themes in this chapter was the word "through." This word would become very important to us, and this chapter would be our constant guide for everything we were going through. It would become so important to us that the word "through" would be the chosen tattoo for our family. I guess that qualifies this text as an important matter in our lives. Here is the text from Isaiah 43.1-3:

> But now, this is what the Lord says, he who created you, Jacob, he who formed you, Israel: "Do not fear, for I have redeemed you; I have summoned you by name; you are mine. When you pass through the waters, I will be with you; and when you pass through the rivers, they will not sweep over you. When you walk through the fire, you will not be burned; the flames will not set you ablaze. For I am the Lord your God, the Holy One of Israel, your Savior."

Read it with great care. And if you're the tattoo type, even choose "through" for your next tattoo. But remember that God says, in the midst of your hardship, suffering, and trial, that "you are mine" (verse 1). This would quickly become our anthem as a family.

God Doesn't Waste Hardship
A controversial worship song came out about two years ago from Hillsong Church in Australia on their Empires recording. The song is entitled "Even When It Hurts (Praise Song)." In the height of Jane's battle with cancer, we were visiting Hillsong Church LA in Southern California, where our oldest son, daughter-in-law, and grandson live.

Since we knew a staff member and he knew about our situation, I had a chance to share our story with the lead pastor, Ben Houston. After the service, he gave Jane and me a copy of the recording since it was just coming out that weekend. Needless to say, it became great strength to us in our situation that Ben took the time to speak faith into our lives.

The cornerstone song on the album for Jane was "Prince of Peace." I can still hear the lines of the song that echoed through our home weekly. Jane loved this song.

> *Your love surrounds me when my thoughts wage war,*
> *When night screams terror, there Your voice will roar,*
> *Come death or shadow, God I know Your light will meet me there.*
> *When fear comes knocking, there You'll be my guard,*
> *When day breeds trouble, there You'll hold my heart,*
> *Come storm or battle, God I know Your peace will meet me there.*

Not only did we have peace in our home through her sickness, we had Peace. However, for me, the track that became my anthem was another tune named "Even When It Hurts (Praise Song)." It seemed to speak the exact language of my heart at the time. I remember telling Ben Houston on another visit I made to Hillsong L.A. after Jane had passed to please tell Joel, his brother who wrote the song, how much this song carried me through Jane's battle.

When Joel got away for months to write this record, I am so glad that God spoke to him and the Spirit authored the specific words to this song. Although it has sparked trivial dialogue with some, it set my heart ablaze with purpose and praise. And as someone who was actually living through hell, the song was not a shock to me like someone who might have never been at that place before. Here is the lyric to a verse and bridge:

> *Take this mountain weight*
> *Take these ocean tears*
> *Hold me through the trial*
> *Come like hope again*
> *Even when the fight seems lost*
> *I'll praise you*
> *Even when it hurts like hell*

I'll praise you
Even when it makes no sense to sing
Louder then I'll sing your praise

Did you catch that? The phrase "even when it hurts like hell" became controversial in the Church. In my travels, I would hear that song led at a Church or youth setting, and that line would be replaced with a more neutered version, losing its power. On Facebook or other social-media platforms, there were threads, arguments, and discourses on why it was wrong to use the word "hell" in a worship song. That was a bit confusing to me. I mean, I understood why. But as a young boy growing up, we would sing much worse language in the hymns of the church I was raised in. There are countless references to "hell" in the hymnal. Why the fuss now?

I'm glad that Joel Houston, the author of the song, chose that one word. It encapsulates everything I was going through. That song didn't need a neutered version of hardship. I think that most people were more concerned with the use of that word than the concept he was talking about. About praising God in your mess.

What I can tell you is that, even while I'm listening to that song while writing this section of the book, there is great emotion. I am taken back to so many memories and discussions between Jane and me. I can feel the presence of God in my writing now that I felt in the pain I was feeling at the time. There was nothing cautious, neutral, or conservative about what we went through. And I didn't need a song that was afraid to speak the truth. The song was challenging me to respond with praise "even when." No matter what I, Job, Paul, or even you are going through today, the response should always be praise.

The degree to which I have uttered the praise of God *in the midst of this hell that I went through is directly related to the* presence of God *that has been with me in this mess.*

As I look back over the last season of my life, it is obvious that God was preparing me for what I was about to go through. It was His way of making sure that there would be no waste in the hardship, suffering, and pain that our family was about to go through.

Just weeks leading up to this point in our life, I was prompted to read the book of Job, as if God were preparing me for what was about to come. And again I found out that God was making sure that I did not place my family before Him or it would be more devastating for me as we walked through Jane's sickness. So many things we might miss in our lives because we are focused upon the little picture, that is, what might be bothering us in the moment. Back out and take a thirty thousand-foot view for a minute. Perspective is the key to playing chess. There isn't as much strategy when you are playing checkers. But if you are playing chess and you can think in layers and how each piece has a distinct value and movement, the strategy is much more involved. We had no doubt that God was playing chess in our lives, uniquely going before us and leading us along the way.

A Story For The Ages

Job's story is one for the ages. And it is similar to the many stories of people in America as well. I think we can all relate very well to it. Maybe you have heard of the statement, "the patience of Job." Or maybe you have heard parts of this ancient story as folklore. Our Western mind-set and entitlement actually add to the narrative of Job. We don't believe that we deserve hardship. We have a great reputation in our community but no character. We have everything we have ever wanted but are not fulfilled. We have a spouse and children but no one to talk to. We have access to the world on our phone and social-media access to hundreds of friends but are lonely. All of us can relate to Job and his story in some way.

However, the most important way that we should relate to Job is how he went through hardship and kept his integrity. When we go through hardship, it will not be our reputation, our stuff we have accumulated, our positions and titles, and our social-media identity that will carry us. When we go through hardship, it will be our relationship with Christ. As His creation and His son or daughter, that will be the most important way we must navigate hardship. Our identity is more about our response during hardship than our response during ease. Because of Job's sense of identity, hardship did not derail or crush him. What is most needed is that our character would match the character of Job so that, when hardship visits, we could assure ourselves the successful walk through hardship to spiritual maturity. Sometimes that requires playing chess and not simply checkers. Just like Job.

A young middle school boy approached me at a summer camp. I thought he was coming to ask me to pray for him. But he was asking if he could pray for me. I told him that he could, and he prayed a beautiful prayer over my family and me. He knew I was going through a hardship, and he wanted to pray for me in my pain.

When he was done praying for me, I asked if I could pray for him. He said yes. And when I asked if there were anything I could pray for, he said yes again. And he told me that his two brothers were killed in the past year, he was living with his mother, and he didn't know his father. Needless to say, we had a great time of prayer together.

But what I learned from this young middle-school boy was that, even in the midst of pain and suffering, if we choose to focus upon God's purposes and not our purposes, it changes our perspective. And we become much more concerned about others than we are for ourselves.

#ifjobhadtwitter If we are going to overcome hardship, suffering, & pain, we must understand that God plays chess while we play checkers

Chapter 4
GRACE IN EVERY STORY

Remember that whatever suffering you are going through, God is using that to build in you a home that He intends to live in.

—C. S. Lewis

Without pressure, there are no diamonds. Let me explain it scientifically. The process in creating diamonds can be done in two main ways: synthetically and naturally. The synthetic process places a cylinder between an anvil and die made from tungsten carbide at a pressure between 5.0 and 7.1 GPa (50,000–70,000 atmospheres) and temperature between 1,200 and 1,500 degrees Celsius. Naturally these conditions occur in limited zones of Earth's mantle about ninety miles below the surface where temperatures rise above 2,000 degrees Fahrenheit (1,050+ degrees Celsius). The pressure-temperature environment for diamond formation and stability is not present globally. But it is thought to be present primarily in the mantle beneath the stable interiors of continental plates (Geology.com).

All of that scientific information is included to say that pressure and temperature are elementary to produce the diamond. One of the most valuable possessions known to humankind requires extreme pressure-temperature before we can enjoy it on all kind of jewelry for our body.

I can't think of too many women who do not want diamonds. However, I doubt they even place thought or care into what kind of pressure-temperature it takes to create one. They simply want to wear it, no matter how it was created.

In the same way, at times, our life is being formed under great pressure and temperature. I mean, think about it. If God wants to dwell in this palace of ours, what is He willing to do to prepare us for His habitation? There is a theme of brokenness and ruin in scripture that is a contrast to how we think in America today. In America, we see hardship as a negative thing. It is a curse. And we avoid hardship. And we don't value hardship for what it can produce in our lives. God understands exactly how much we can take, and He will not overbear us with weight. He will use the pressure and temperature in our lives to produce something of great value if we let Him. The strength that He gives us is His presence and His grace, which is the protection against all of the pressure and temperature in our lives. Once the dirty piece of coal is forged under great pressure, the beauty can be seen. There is always grace in every story.

If we do not value the process of hardship, it can lead to many things. Of course, there are other reasons. And we will look at those throughout the book. But in this chapter, let's look at hardship and its role in our palace. Ultimately devaluing hardship can lead to us blaming God or others for hardship and trying to avoid any form of it in our lives. And in so doing, we miss an opportunity of receiving from one of the great teachers of life. Why? God uses hardship, suffering, and pain for His purposes and our maturity. So by not seeing His presence in the pain, we lose sight of the big picture. And by not seeing His grace in the pain, we miss a great opportunity to mature through trial.

The Empire Not Made With Hands
I believe that God is so concerned about our welfare, even when it doesn't look like it. Why? There are many reasons. His greatest attribute is love,

and the trait of love defines Him. We are His children, and He loves His children. And God is so concerned with our welfare because His Son had to go through such hardship, suffering, and pain in order to take ours. And still, yet another way of God's thinking about us is that His ways are not our ways, and His thoughts are not our thoughts.

But He has something in mind beyond our imagination, and He must be trusted. One of the least talked about truths in scripture of why God cares for us so much is because we are God's building, His abode, and the habitation and dwelling place of His presence. Literally, we are His empire, a place that is under a single supreme authority. His Spirit does not live in a material temple made with hands. He dwells in each of us.

Matthew 7 symbolizes our lives as a home and describes the elements that beat against our home. Hebrews 3 speaks of the concept of God's children being His house. And 1 Corinthians 3 also speaks of this concept of us being His field and His building, the place where He lives. Maybe one of the key reasons why God is so concerned about us is because He is so interested in us as His possession. And He loves His house. He loves you and me and is completely aware of every storm, wind, rain, and intruder that comes against His house. It can be easy to see all of the elements that beat against our home as pain, injustice, and unfair. But if we will allow our homes to be built upon the solid rock of Christ as our foundation, nothing will be able to beat against our home and knock it down.

One of the things that has been a practice in our home is playing music, especially worship. My kids would often ask me to get a new playlist because I would play my favorite songs so much. Over the last season, as we were going through everything in our home, we would often turn up the music and turn our empire into His palace. Through everything we were going through, there was a constant presence in our lives, and we knew it. We never felt like our home was empty. We never felt despair or hopelessness.

We never felt like we were alone. Because we decided how we were going to go through this. We did not let the circumstances dictate our attitude. We were going to let our attitude dictate our circumstances.

What we felt is that God was so interested in us that He would never leave us. We felt His presence as a shadow. His presence was a song turned up quite loud. His presence was a family member or friends who would come over to help us clean or to serve Jane and give me a break. We especially felt His presence in our empire when so many meals were brought to us that we had no place to put the food. We felt His presence in our lives because we made an intentional effort to focus upon God's presence in our lives and not the pain. We allowed His authority in our empire. We welcomed His authority in our empire. And He never disappoints to come when asked.

Take A Moment Now

I want you to do that now. I dare you. Even if you are at work or school or in a public place, turn the music up, or just silence everything that is going on. Close your eyes. And invite His presence into your life while you are reading this. Say it verbally. Invite God to walk into the room and to bring His peace, power, and presence into your home, workplace, or school. Trust me, if you will do this, everything will change. Your attitude and focus will change, and those are the two most formative things in your life that produce atmosphere and culture. Your thinking and your sight are powerful contributors to either depression and despair or rejoicing and relaxation. If you are buried in debt, sick in your body, worried about your children, or struggling with your self-image because you didn't get 100 'likes' or if your family is falling apart, invite God into your life right now. I have no doubts that He will be known in a real way.

A classic little book was written almost thirty years ago on the life of Brother Lawrence, a devout and pious author who lived in the mid-1600s. The book was called *The Practice of the Presence of God*. Brother Lawrence was converted to Christianity as a teenager. The moment that brought his conversion was a vision he had of the providence of God. Here is how his conversion is described in the first chapter of the book:

> *in the winter, seeing a tree stripped of its leaves, and considering that within a little time, the leaves would be renewed, and after that the flowers and fruit would then appear, he received a high view of the Providence and Power of GOD, which has never since been effaced from his soul. Not even in Winter.*

See, Brother Lawrence began his pursuit of God by seeing a vision of the winter condition of the trees around him. But not only did he see them as sticks and branches void of leaves or fruit, he saw them with the hope of spring renewal. Wow! Every time I read this little book, I am challenged by the simplicity of the moment that a teenager was transformed by a vision of winter and spring, of practicing His presence, no matter what the weather. This is something that became a practice for us. We would often play a song for each other, and our excitement would lift the mood of the home, the report, or the doctor's appointment that we just had. We would pray through recordings that were given to us by friends or from our favorite artists. I'm sure, if you look at my playlist right now, there are songs that would show hundreds of plays.

One of those moments took place shortly after Jane passed. I was sitting in my living room in a Minnesota winter. I was alone again and feeling somewhat sorry for myself and missing my best friend. And I felt the loneliness and the despair of my situation falling upon me. I immediately recognized what was happening to me and how much Satan probably wanted me to quit right then. But I wasn't going to let my circumstances dictate my mood or thoughts. I played two songs. I have told the story of the first song here in this book and how much this song meant to me. So I played "Even When It Hurts (Praise Song)" for over an hour, and my mood changed as I sung the words and worshiped God with my whole heart.

I had a choice to make in that moment, and to be honest, I had many other moments just like that in the first year going through Jane's death. And I was creating a pattern in my life. The worship came from my my lips first. And then it came from my heart, even if it took about ten times through the song. But it sure beat sitting in anger, confusion, bitterness, apathy, or doubt. And every time I disciplined myself to worship, the presence of God followed by filling my apartment, my car, the plane, or the hotel. And immediately the pain was gone.

That day, when I was finished with the first song, I played a second one. And I know that everyone heard this one. How can anyone not be moved by the praise song from Chris Tomlin, "God's Great Dance Floor." That beat became my neighbor's rhythm many times, I'm sure, as I turned up and danced upon my problems singing,

I'm coming back to the start, where you found me,
I'm coming back to your heart, now I surrender.
Take me, this is all I can bring.

You'll never stop loving us
No matter how far we run,
You'll never give up on us,
All of heaven shouts let the future begin.

I feel alive, I come alive
I am alive on God's great dance floor

I'm not telling you this is easy. But I am telling you that this makes everything else easier. And I'm telling you it's the right thing to do, like

Paul and Silas who were imprisoned in Philippi. The story is told in Acts 16. Because Paul and Silas were seeing great things happen in the city and many were upset with them, they were unfairly charged and brought before the magistrate. The magistrate had them stripped naked, beaten with rods, shackled, and imprisoned in the inner prison that was anything unlike the regular prison cells. But as Luke tells the story in Acts 16, everyone heard singing coming from the prison around midnight. It was coming from the inner cell, where conditions were the worst. What followed was God's presence in an earthquake. And the doors fell off the cell, and they walked out rejoicing.

Try remaining in a bad mood while worshipping. Try focusing upon all of your problems while reading the Word. Try giving up while you are creating a thank list of all of the things God has done for you. It worked for Paul, Silas, Job, and me. And it will work for you.

Here's an exercise I want you to do right now while reading the book. Your hand is your problem. Write your problem on your hand. Or put a small piece of paper in your hand with your problem written on it. And do this little exercise as a symbol of focusing upon the right thing.

> *If you place your hand right in front of your face, you will not be able to see, but if you extend your hand away from your face, you will be able to see clearly. It's just a few inches of movement. And everything is clearer. Try that while you are reading, and you will not get very far. Try it while you are running, and you will slam into an object really fast. Please don't try it while you are driving.*

In the same way, if your hand is the problem in your life, by placing it in front of your face, you can only focus on the problem, and you will see nothing else. But if you will take your hand away from your face, even just the length of your arm, you will be able to see clearly past your problem. I believe that God is sovereign and can redeem anything that we are going through. And He has promised that He will show up when asked. Psalm 91 is a classic chapter in the Old Testament that invites the presence of God into the darkness and the gloom and the death of our situations. And it promises His presence in many symbolic ways. Read it and sense the presence of the Holy Spirit in your setting immediately.

God Is Not Intimidated By Darkness

If you look at what is going on in America you will see a lot of darkness. But, darkness is where God does His best work. The place of my pain becomes the place of His presence. Where He turns our mess into His message. Where our chaos is placed on His canvas and He creates a masterpiece. Where tragedy is really the road to triumph. Where hardship becomes history. God does His greatest work in the midst of our greatest need. Try as we might to paint a different picture, we live in a broken palace, where God is the landlord.

God is not intimidated by darkness, humanism, or moral relativity. He is not intimidated by the sexual revolution, the destruction of the family, or the social-media phenomenon. God does His best work in the midst of our darkest moment. Just because the condition of society and the statistics in our land are overwhelmingly leaning toward a nation out of control or your own life is out of control, it doesn't mean that God is worried or out of control. We need a better picture of God if we are going to handle the hardship in our world and our life. Some of us in the church spend more time trying to help God do His job than we do trusting Him as the boss.

I don't think that God is up in heaven, seated on His throne with His head buried in His hands and shaking His head. I don't think that Jesus is up in heaven, seated on the right hand of God with His head rolled back in disbelief at what is going on in our nation. And I don't think that the Holy Spirit is here on the earth, walking around with His head down and a frown on His face, wondering what His next steps are going to be to counter Satan. No, that is not the picture I have of the Trinity. I believe God can handle anything.

He flung worlds into existence with His words. He set the borders of the seas and told them how far they could recede. He hung stars and planets in the sky and ordered the laws of nature so that space and world could exist together. He created the human body with its intricacies and scientific mysteries and breathed life into each of us for a period of time on the earth. Do you actually think He is intimidated by racism, violence, and self-harm? Do you think that your debt, broken relationships, or sickness is too difficult for Him? God is powerful enough to be our Creator, and He is present enough to be our peace.

Most people will focus upon the pain in their life. I have chosen to focus upon His presence in mine. People who have gone through so much brokenness, ruin, pain, and destruction can become great examples of Christianity. It's how God works. We become His display, the displays of His good works and grace. Although we try to avoid trials and complain in times of difficulty, these times will test the patterns and the disciplines we are making. Are we inviting God's presence into our situation or repelling Him with our attitude? If we are going through a hardship, we are a candidate for His presence. He is drawn to dire situations and dark moments. We are in line to receive His grace to help in time of need. Every situation has the same amount of pain and God because He is present in it all.

During the 9/11 terrorist attacks, certainly the most terrifying days of our nation's history, Anne Graham Lotz said, "Maybe the answer to the question, 'Where was God during 9/11' is really easy. Maybe He did as we asked Him as a nation. Maybe He stayed away from our nation, and our schools, and our government, just like we have asked Him." I know what she is saying, almost trying to concede the question. But let me tell you what I believe about God and 9/11 or any other tragedy you might be going through today.

I believe that God can work immediately in the mess, or, faithfully in the process. Immediately with His miracle. Or faithfully with His presence. I believe that God is still on the throne and all sufficient and powerful. And I believe He is present in every matter if we want Him to be. And I believe He still heals today miraculously and is still present today faithfully. You will be able to read many healings in our story here in this book. You will see undeniable stories of God and His interruption in many lives in our ministry. But I believe that you can also see God and His presence giving strength to you in the process.

Looking at 9/11, we saw God working both ways. In the first responders running into the chaos of a burning building to save more lives. Or the countless stories of people who testified that they should have been dead but were spared by a miracle. And maybe He is giving wisdom to the doctor in the operating room trying to save your relative from cancer. And maybe He is giving shelter to your child in the car accident who might be injured but should have died. Don't you think that, if God were present at the beginning of time creating the stars, the oceans, and our humanity, He is still present in our daily lives and willing to turn anything into His perfect will for our lives, if we ask Him to. See, He can handle anything, if He is allowed to.

Take a look at another person in the Old Testament who went through a tremendous amount of hardship. And if we understand his story completely, I'm sure most of us would concede that Joseph went through these hardships unjustly after being betrayed by his brothers, thrown into a pit to die, sold to a mob, placed in prison, unjustly accused of adultery, and then placed back into prison. After all of that, here's what Joseph said to his brothers when they came to visit him. In Genesis 50.19–20, he says, "Do not be afraid, for am I in God's place? As for you, you meant evil against me, but God meant it for good in order to bring about this present result, to preserve many people alive." Wow. Talk about perspective. Look at this verse more completely.

The first part of this text is an amazing admission. God has Joseph in the right place, even if that location isn't very comfortable. When we are able to say that God is sovereign enough to position us as He sees fit for His plan, we set ourselves up to go through hardship with success. And then look at the middle portion of what Joseph says about the cause of his hardship. He admitted that what went on in his life was the fault of his brothers, not God. How many things happen in our life are simply cause and effect? Life, in the form of other people's decisions, or accidents, or even sickness, just happens. It's at the fault or blame of no one. Life needs to be lived, and sometimes it takes a little effort from us.

> *We must remove the thinking that life is math, that it can be added up and worked like an equation. Life is not math. Life is art. It takes flexibility, and it is beautiful in the eye of the beholder.*

No Pain, No Gain

Athletes know the principle well. If they practice, lift weights, do cardio and muscle memory repetitions, and remember their wellness and nutrition, the discipline from these things will increase their chances to be a champion. It's not easy. But it is worth it. The old saying "no pain, no gain" is a reality that some people experience. But most people never have a chance to know. As we look at our family's story, Job's situation, and other accounts from the Bible on the matter of discipline, we are learning the importance of trusting the process and the presence of grace in our difficulty. It can be easy to look solely upon the pain in a story while we are in the long process. But at the same time, we should not miss the presence in the story, as God is working His will in our situation.

Because I played multiple sports, I have seen the return on investment. As an avid basketball player still today, I can remember practice. I can still feel the burn in my lungs, the intensity in my mind, and the soreness in my body during and after practice. It wasn't even the game. I can recall walking into youth group on Wednesday evenings with wet hair because I had just left practice and got a quick shower at school so I could get to Church.

My parents had one rule with our sports. We could play all the sports we want, but we couldn't miss Church. Sports and faith were an easy synergy for me because of this. There were so many lessons I shared between my athletics and my faith. And the gain from pain was foremost. It seemed the coaches had embodied the idea that the games would be easy because practice is tougher. I'm not sure I liked that much as a player because there were four and sometimes five practices each week and only one or two games. And the fans—okay, the girls—only came to the games!

Playing sports all of my life, I know the excitement of pregame nerves, game pressure, and postgame laughter or tears. The investment was painful most of the time. But the return was worth the hours, failures, pain, travel, running, lifting, and losses. And it was certainly worth the excitement, baskets, stops, crowd, cheerleaders, team relationships, and wins. What we cannot do is focus simply on the pain or the losses of a situation in our lives. We have to focus on the presence and the wins in the situation. Wins at game time happen because of wins at practice times. We have to value the difficulty of practice if we are ever going to enjoy the victory in competition.

To Buffet Or Not To Buffet

I have learned another lesson from Paul. He said in chapter 9 of the second letter to the Corinthians that "we buffet our body and handle it roughly and bring it into submission so that after we have preached to others we cannot be disqualified." In this same chapter, he is dealing with the principle of discipline and examination in many areas, including our stewardship in the area of eating, relationships, teaching, war, farming, and finally the athletic arena.

While too many of us have chosen to sit at the table and buffet our body, we must remember that is not the word Paul is using here. The buffet at your local Chinese restaurant is not what Paul is calling us to. Instead he uses the word "buffeting" our body or the term "beat," "bruise," or "bring our body into submission." The Greek word Paul used is *hupo-piazow*, which literally means to focus the discipline to an area and beat it black and blue. That is the kind of focus it takes to overcome selfishness, to bring our life into discipline, to focus upon my self-leadership. One of the great lessons of leadership is not leading others. But leading yourself. If we want to see the difficulties that we are going through actually turn out for our good, it will require the discipline, commitment, and dedication of soldiers, athletes, and farmers we referenced earlier (2 Tim. 2.4–6). Are you looking at the pain of your situation or the presence of your Savior?

He walked up to me at a youth group, and it was obvious he had some physical and mental issues. He couldn't balance, and he had headaches often. Much of the time, he could see spots in his vision, all because of psychedelic drugs he had been doing for years. But after the students prayed for him, he began to walk around and actually run through the auditorium without pain and any imbalance or sight issues. God had healed him instantly.

As he finished his remarkable parade around the room, he came back up to the front where I was standing. He was overtaken with emotion and so grateful. I asked him to say a few words to the students. But he could not. He was so overwhelmed by the grace of God to heal him and the presence of God in the room that he was just crying. God's presence is always more important than our pain.

When is the last time you simply couldn't move on? When you were overwhelmed by thanksgiving for what God has done in your life?

#ifjobhadtwitter Most people will choose to focus upon the pain in their life. But I have chosen to focus upon His presence in my life.

Chapter 5
DON'T DO HARDSHIP ALONE

Don't be the person who complains about
suffering like it only belongs to them.

—Chinese proverb

"No man is an island." John Donne wrote this in dealing with suffering and sickness. He wrote this in 1624 while going through a life-threatening sickness yet continuing to preach and lead his congregation. The message of the short poem was to urge his congregation to be connected to each other in times of hardship. Donne was an inspirational pastor whose poem has been quoted outside the religious setting and may even be more popular in the arts and poetic setting. But beyond a poetical writing, it is a critical lesson for the Church to learn.

Hardship, suffering, and pain have no respect to race, gender, economic status, age group, or religious background. If you are breathing, it is going to happen to you. Don't be the person who complains about suffering like he or she is the only person who is experiencing it. Instead of living in denial, do hardship with someone. In this chapter, I want you to see the role that others play in our suffering and ultimately in our healing. In the past year, people have asked me what are my greatest lessons learned in this season. I'm sure that one of the things I have said to almost everyone is, "You should never do hardship alone." Job learned this great lesson also, the hard way.

After Job had lost everything, we find him sitting alone outside the town near a dump. It was in one of the lowest moments of his life. He had been smitten with sores all over his body, and he was tending to his wounds as his friends came up to him. The scriptures say they could hardly recognize him, and they began to weep. Job's three friends sat next to him for an entire week and didn't say a word. They simply cried with him and tended to him.

Satan had taken Job's children, his servants, his cattle, his ranch, and now his health. Job's wife turned on him because of this. She had told him to curse God and die. There is no way out. Job was experiencing such great pressure from everywhere.

In this condition, as Job was seated with his friends, something interesting takes place. A dialogue that takes up more than twenty chapters is recorded as Job talks with his friends about suffering, justice, and hardship. These remarkable conversations are like our attempt to understand the same things. They are not very successful.

One of his friends tells Job it is his fault. Another tells Job that he is not righteous enough. In their conversations, we see men asking Job what he has done to receive this treatment. It all seems so wrong, even though their intentions were right. Sometimes I think that we must learn to be still and not struggle with our attempts to explain God or His ways. Look at the direction of the questions they asked Job. Each asked Job what he did wrong or what he hadn't done right. However, this is not the right question. We will deal with the right questions to ask in another chapter.

The problem is that, when you ask the wrong question, you will not get the right answer. Job's story was not about sin or looking for someone to blame. His story wasn't about what he did right or wrong during the hardship. And that is something we must all learn. Just because you are going through a difficulty, it doesn't mean that you have done something wrong. Or on the other hand, you have not done something right. And Job's friends teach us a great lesson about how to walk through hardship with someone.

Being a presence-based friend in crisis is powerful. It's something that Job's friends should have done. They were off to a great start by sitting with him for seven days in silence. The problems began when they opened their mouths and began to give him their thoughts on matters they had never been through. I learned this lesson many years ago at the beginning of my ministry. It was the summer of 1985, and I walked into the first crisis in my ministry as a young youth pastor.

Jesse Was Fighting For His Life

The first Church I had worked in out of college was in Indiana. I had only been in this church for three months. We had just finished a series of messages in our youth group on evangelism called "We Are the Church." It was a twist on the 1985 project, "We Are the World," a multi-artist cause to raise money for Africa. We had given our students T-shirts and sent them to school and their world with the message, "America for Jesus."

The next day, Thursday, I received a phone call from the family of a graduating senior boy in our youth ministry. He was on his way to college to study for ministry that fall and was the backbone of the youth ministry. He had become a very close friend, and we were spending a lot of time talking about youth ministry.

As his father was crying on the phone, I realized I was in over my head. He began to tell me that his son Jesse had just been flown to Indianapolis Children's Hospital because he had fallen out of a vehicle at work. When

I heard this, I knew I needed to be with the family. I hung up from that frantic call and then realized that my lead pastor was not in the office that day and I was going to handle everything myself. I left a message at his home because we did not have cell phones then and drove to Indianapolis. On the way to the hospital, I had no clue what to do. They didn't teach us those things thirty years ago in college.

When I got to the hospital, I walked into the waiting room to meet the family. But what I didn't realize was how bad the situation was. As the father was updating me about Jesse's condition, I realized Jesse was in a fight for his life. The doctors had given him only hours to live. And here I was with this family, trying to figure out what to say. As the father finished telling me what had happened, the mother and two young siblings walked over and began to cry. The only thing I could think of was to simply go to the group hug.

Trust me. I am so glad that worked. We stood there as a family and youth pastor hugging for at least ten minutes. I think I was relieved that I didn't have to say anything. I'm not sure I could have thought of something to say in that moment.

There were no words of wisdom or revelation and nothing I could say in that moment that could change the situation. I just remember being at peace while hugging them, crying with them, and saying nothing. After a while, I did think to pray with them. That was remarkably easy. As I said, I'd only been in that church about three months. I really did not even know the family very well. But in these moments in the hospital, we were bonding and becoming very close without saying many words. I simply cried and sat with them and served them until my pastor showed up a few hours later and had everything right to say.

Jessie passed away that night, and I would eventually walk them through the next few weeks and months. In one of our conversations months after the funeral, the parents told me that what meant the most to them in those moments in the hospital was my presence in that group hug. They didn't need my theological discussion in that moment. They needed me to cry with them and to sit with them and simply listen. To be honest, for a moment, when they told me how much my silence meant to them, I thought I was a genius. But then I realized I wasn't a genius. I really didn't know what to say in the moment.

Job Had Great Friends Until They Opened Their Mouth

It's not that we have nothing to say. It's just that we need to know when to say it. We need to be as willing to sit with someone as we are to speak with someone. I think that is exactly what Job needed. And that is what you and I need too. Job's situation was not about theological discussions or cured statements about wisdom from friends who had never been through the water or the fire. It was about being a friend. It was more about trust and seeing God in the midst of our suffering. Job had great friends until they opened their mouth. Don't underestimate silence.

As Job's friends are finished speaking with him, God steps in and talks to the friends. This is a remarkable conversation. It is recorded in chapter 42 at the end of the book. After God was done speaking with Job, he says to his friends in verse 7,

> It came about after the LORD had spoken these words to Job, that the LORD said to Eliphaz the Temanite, "My wrath is kindled against you and against your two friends, because you have not spoken of Me what is right as My servant Job has. Now therefore, take for yourselves seven bulls and seven rams, and go to My servant Job, and offer up a burnt offering for yourselves, and My servant Job will pray for you. For I will accept him so that I may not do with you according to your folly, because you have not spoken of Me what is right, as My servant Job has.

God was saying to these friends that they should have listened to Job. It was Job who was handling the situation the right way. Job didn't need their words. He needed their friendship. And God even says to them that they should go apologize to Job.

Maybe people have told you there is no hope in the midst of your situation. Perhaps you have even had a visit from someone like Job's friends who has told you that you did something wrong or you haven't done something right. They are well meaning. But if someone hasn't experienced hardship, it is very difficult to hear from his or her perspective if you are in the midst of suffering he or she does not understand.

Listen. The conversations need to happen. I think we can learn a lot through exploratory thought. But sometimes, like Job, we have great friends until they open their mouth. Maybe it is better that we just sit with each other and not try to understand God's sovereignty. Or to answer questions that only He has the answers for.

In the Old Testament, Solomon wrote in Ecclesiastes 4.9–10, "Two are better than one, because they have a good return for their work. If one falls down, his friend can help him up. But pity the man who falls and has no one to help him up!"

What a great reminder to make sure that we have the right squad or posse or tribe or crew around us. We should never do hardship alone. I remember so many moments that taught our family about friendship. Let me tell you about a few of the people who came alongside us and made the difference in our hardship.

The Specialist Doctor in the Emergency Department
The night we went into the hospital, there was a doctor who had years of experience in what we were going through. He became a trusted friend to us over the next year. We really didn't even see him more than

monthly, but our relationship with him was built on trust and a divine chess move on God's part to have him there the night we went to the hospital. He was the doctor who started everything off on the right foot and assigned the right team to us who would oversee Jane's care for the next sixteen months.

A Woman Who had Lost Her Father to Cancer

Sometimes you get a visitor who teaches you something you really didn't want to hear. A woman who had lost her father to cancer came to speak with us and recounted the sad loss in her life. She was there to comfort us, but it didn't seem like it at the time.

That visit shaped a very important principle in Jane and me. When she left the room, after telling us the story of the death of her father, I remember talking to Jane about how we were not going to talk like that. We were not going to have those discussions. We were going to speak life over our situation. And that visit shaped how courageously we would speak to each other as we went through this battle. It was a lesson we didn't see at the time, but was very important to how we would go through our hardship.

The Pastor's Kid (PK) Nurses Who Served Us

Anyone who really knows us very well understands that we love the PK's. While we were at the hospital, this became a pattern. We had three separate nurses who served us who were pastor kids (PKs). One of them even attended our Church and became very important in our process. Every time we would see her, our hearts were lifted. I can say that we never really even had deep theological discussions with these nurses. There were times when they would just sit with Jane. At times, they would just serve her. And there were many times when they would pray for us before they would leave their shift or walk with me and just talk. The professionalism and the compassion from these PK friends was calming and faith-filling to us.

College Students and the Prayer Meeting at Our Home

It was just a week before Jane was to have a major blood test. And Jane wanted to have a prayer meeting. So we called a few of the students who were close to us from a nearby Christian university. These students came to our condo in downtown Minneapolis and carried our burden. What was so moving to us in this moment was that, after thirty-four years of ministry and work with young people, now they were returning the ministry to us in the most important time of our life.

I remember looking around during the prayer meeting at the students and being overcome with emotion because I could see God assembling these students and they would be a major part of our story.

Shortly after the prayer meeting, we would receive news that Jane's diagnosed level of melanoma in her blood dropped from 71 percent to 0 percent in just a few weeks. She had gone from a diagnosis of 71 percent, which was almost unheard of, to a level of 0 percent. As told later in this book, our doctors were sure this was not simply the prescribed drugs she was on. The chemotherapy was not aggressive enough to impact her cancer that quickly. We believe she was healed and given more time to complete what God wanted to do in Jane's life. And these students had everything to do with this moment in our life.

When Jorie Walked into the Room After Her Honeymoon

One of the great moments of our time in the hospital was when Jorie walked into the ICU when she returned from her honeymoon. Because Jane and I went directly to the hospital the night of the wedding, we did not see Jorie and Luke until that moment. And through the week while we were battling the diagnosis and they were on their honeymoon, we did not share much with them because we wanted them to enjoy this moment in their life. But we knew that we could not mask everything, and Jorie could tell something was wrong. She would try to call several times a day, and

I was running out of excuses on why she couldn't talk with her mom and that we were fine and Mom was just exhausted.

But the morning Jorie walked into the ICU and saw Jane with all of the wires and machines attached to her was one of the most emotional moments of my life as they hugged and cried together. When they were done hugging and crying together, Jorie prayed and set the room straight with her lioness attitude and fierce faith. I really believe she was standing in that room holding a sword and was ready to fight. I remember thinking in that moment of the many times my kids showed us through the years that they actually had a faith of their own. It wasn't my faith or Jane's faith. It was their faith.

Our Angel in the Clouds

I'm sure that some people will find this a little emotionally charged and somewhat of a reach. But on the twenty-sixth day of Jane's second stay in the hospital, we were up on the observation deck and talking and preparing to leave the next morning. As we were looking into the sky, Jane noticed a cloud formation and became very excited. The clouds had formed an almost perfect shape of an angel. From the top of its head flowing with long hair, its long body covered by a robe, and arms extended to the side in the shape of a cross, this sign mesmerized us. We knew that God would never leave us or forsake us. It was the last picture in our minds of His faithfulness and presence in our lives. That heavenly visitor was one of the most encouraging moments in our early battle. This moment was captured and placed on Jane's social-media pages on August 28, 2015, as proof. She posted these words with the photo, "He will command His angels concerning you to guard you in all of your ways" (Ps. 91.11). It was just a few months before she would pass into heaven and meet that messenger.

A Word from an Intercessor in Australia

Jane worked for about four years for one of the pastors at our church. He happens to be from Australia and grew up in the Hillsong Church in

Sydney. At his request, one of the lead intercessors in the Hillsong Church placed Jane on their global prayer list. And the lead intercessor even cited Jane's situation in one of his posts on social media. That personal relationship produced thousands of people who were praying for us.

I'm not sure how people deal with hardship without their faith, let alone, a church. So much good happens through the local church, and so much inspiration happens in a personal faith in God. Jane wrote in her journal just three months before she passed,

> *Community releases the love that empowers us to continue to hold onto the hope beyond reason.*

It's one of my favorite notes from her journal. The power of the global church (the community) brought Jane's first healing and helped us to hold onto hope beyond that healing until her ultimate death.

When Our Pastors Walked into the Room

In the last few days of Jane's battle, when she was in and out of consciousness, our pastoral leaders organized a visit to the home. Seven of our closest minister friends from around the Twin Cities came over on the same night to read and pray with us. Along with these was our family. Think about that. Some of the godliest people in our lives were standing with us one more time. That night became a statement on how we were going to finish this battle.

Believing that God was going to do a miracle, we all prayed one more time. Without a shadow of doubt, I instructed all of them that we were not saying good-bye. We were praying for a supernatural healing. At the end of the prayer meeting, I explained to Jane, who was in the room, and what we had just done. Her reply? She looked around the room and said to all of us in a faint voice, "There are angels here also." Nobody in that room doubted it, and we knew that none of us was alone in the room.

All of the People Who Brought Us Meals

Anyone who has ever been on the receiving end of a food tree or women's ministry meal list will attest to the impact of receiving weeks of meals, notes, and visits from generous friends and strangers. Our refrigerator was packed for months. But it was more than the food that our family and friends brought to us. Sometimes they would stay and talk, help clean, or even shop for us and pick up a few things that we needed. There were also times when we never met the person who brought a meal or a gift card for us to buy a meal that night. We never knew the people who took hours to prepare a meal, leave their family to drive it over to us, and spend their own money. And they would never get to sit and pray with us or hear us say "thank you." These people were doing this because they were serving God and not us. And the power of the nameless ones is still humbling today when I think about it a year and a half later.

One final friend made my life easier at this time. Doing hardship is something all of us will have to experience someday. Hopefully we will each have moments like these in the middle of our suffering. I think maybe Job's friends could have taken a lesson from this youth pastor friend of mine. Sometimes the best friend says nothing.

Some friends know exactly what not to say.

As I continued to travel part time while Jane was sick, many times people would affirm us as we were going through this battle. People would pray, give me a word of encouragement, or even hand me a gift of some kind. But there was one moment in particular when friendship was overwhelming to me. It had been a rough week, and I was leaving Jane for the weekend. There was always someone in our family who would stay with her in these times, but it still wasn't easy for me to not be there.

On this occasion, I remember getting off the plane exhausted and emotional from everything that was going on. But ministry doesn't stop, and I was looking forward to getting to the hotel and spending some time alone to recharge for the three days of meetings. And as I walked out of the airport to meet the youth pastor, he simply walked up to me and hugged me. He said nothing. Then he pulled away, and we got into the car. It was the most respectful and graceful greeting I had ever received. To this day, neither of us has said anything to each other about the moment. To be honest, nothing needed to be said.

#ifjobhadtwitter I had great friends until they opened their mouth. The presence of friends is sometimes more important than their words.

Chapter 6
THE UNIVERSITY OF SUFFERING

If you want to hear the truth, you must let suffering speak.

—Cornel West

Most of us do not like our teachers for various reasons. I remember when I was in middle school and the teacher was out of the room for the first five minutes of biology class. We did not like this teacher because he was strict. It had nothing to do with whether we were learning from him, how smart he was, or how good of a teacher he was. But he was strict. And we were in middle school.

We walked into class that day and saw the teacher wrote on the board that he would be back in five minutes. And he left us instructions. Written in simple plain English were the words "Water Plant." Now we had two plants in the room, a large biology class plant at the front of the room that was bigger than life. It was everyone's favorite and probably five feet tall. But another plant was in the room. And his name was Bill Plant, a sixth grader. And you are already ahead of me. A few of us went to the front, got the watering pail, and did exactly what our teacher was instructing us to do. It was written in plain English on the board. So we watered the Plant, soaked him, messed with him a little, and then placed the pail back at the front of the room.

As Bill Plant started to leave the room and go to the bathroom to get cleaned up, the teacher walked in. And this is what we didn't like about our teacher. He was not happy, and the group of us who took his instruction was sent to the principal's office.

Jesus Was A Teacher

A teacher is one of the most important persons in our culture. Do you know that Jesus was a teacher? God is a rabbi. God is a teacher. Have you ever thought about that? I don't think anyone is smarter than God. He is always the smartest person in every room. Having the right people in the room can really change how we deal with difficulty. We just learned that every discussion we have on hardship is better if it is collaborative and involves multiple people. Submitting to someone who is much smarter than we are is very important. It can quicken our learning curve, save us a mass amount of time learning something, and add years to our life! So what is God's advice to Job? If we are willing to look at God's conversations with Job, we can learn a lot about His views on hardship, suffering, and pain.

When I was in Israel, one of the most intriguing things I learned was the rabbi-student relationship. On one of the days visiting Old Jerusalem, as I walked through the streets, I noticed a rabbi and his students walking through the streets of Israel. The commitment of the students to stay very close to the rabbi moved me. There was an obvious trust between the students and the rabbi. It was a unique relationship. Wherever he went, they went. If he stopped, they stopped. If he went into a shop, they went into a shop. And when he stopped and sat by the side of the street, each of them sat down and began to listen to him. It was their classroom, and he was the teacher. I don't remember hearing them say a word. They were listening to the rabbi.

And one of the thoughts I had while standing across the street watching this was, *These guys must have it nice. They don't have to make any decisions on their own!* Anything they need could be received from the rabbi—wisdom, knowledge, teachings, insight on all of their questions, and guidance in their life. They had an instant Wikipedia or Google search or hangout at their fingertips. I found this while doing my Graduate Studies about the educational levels in the United States:

> *According to the US Census Bureau in 2014, 88% of Americans have graduated from High School or have received their GED. Furthermore, about 32% of Americans have graduated with a Bachelor's degree from College. The US Census Bureau reported that about 12% of people have graduated with a Master's degree. Finally, the report shows that about 4% of Americans have accomplished a Doctoral degree or terminal degree in field of some form. So, looking at this data, about 48% of Americans have completed a University degree of some form. That is almost half.*

Education has its place in our society. But what about the School of Hard Knocks, as they say?

School Of Hard Knocks

Most of us have at least attended the School of Hard Knocks. Maybe some of you are a resident at this school while others are merely commuters. How long we remain in this school probably depends on how quickly we learn. Do you remember when Rafiki is talking with Simba in *The Lion King*? As they are talking, Rafiki smacks Simba over the head with his stick. He is trying to teach him a lesson. And Simba gets very upset with him for hitting him over the head. As they continue talking, Rafiki swings his stick at Simba again to see if he is learning anything. Simba ducks without hesitancy, avoiding the pain of being smacked on the head again by Rafiki's stick.

And Rafiki responds to Simba, "Aha, see, you learn."

And much like Rafiki's stick, hardship continues to come at us. If God is so loving, how can He allow famine or poverty? If God is so fair, why do innocent people suffer? If God is so powerful, why can He not rid the world of sickness? Until we come to a settlement with these questions, we will continue to be hit over the head, just like Simba.

Have you ever thought about a graduate degree in suffering? Probably not. Our personal theology of comfort cannot allow for any kind of inequity in our life. That's not how we think in America. But because hardship exists, we have to rethink as Americans. It will be a constant theme in this book. We must be willing to unlearn things we have been taught all of our lives. In a society that offers warranties, guarantees, and satisfaction guaranteed or your money-back incentives, we have become spoiled with lifestyle perfection. And anything that doesn't fit into our comfortable Western mentality is dismissed as injustice or curse. This thinking easily shrugs off hard knocks as deplorable and avoidable when what we should be thinking about instead is how we can turn hard knocks into an opportunity for our growth, how to turn difficulty into an opportunity for a strong mind, and how to turn difficulty into an opportunity for developing greater perseverance and maturity. Our default thinking toward difficulty is to avoid hardship, suffering, and pain altogether. And so, we must develop a reset in our thinking that will allow for hard knocks and turn it into our good.

One of the chapters of the book of Job has been a focal point of my prayers. Job 5 is one of Job's friends talking to Job about how God can turn every situation around. Whoa. It's some great stuff to think about if you are in the middle of a trial. I want to do a quick commentary with a few verses in Job 5.

"Behold, happy is the man whom God corrects; Therefore, do not despise the chastening of the Almighty" (Job 5.17). You wouldn't think that hardship and difficulty would be synonymous with a happy day. But Job is assured that, when the Almighty does the chastening, all things must be taken with a smile on our face, knowing that His will in the end will be good. And this position will result in a happy disposition. Do you see chastening as a tool to correction and maturity? The warning from God is to not run from it or despise it, but to embrace it and smile.

"For He bruises, but He binds up; He wounds, but His hands make whole" (Job 5.18). Looking at what is going on in your life (depression, relational issues, bad grades, financial difficulty, family problems, and so on) can be overwhelming. We have caused some of these things, others have influenced a few of these things, many of these things just happened in the course of life, and perhaps God caused others of these things. Understanding that God is in control of the chaos will give the hurt and the loneliness a purpose. You have to believe that He knows what He is doing. In the end, He will personally turn the hurt into wholeness with His own hands. He will turn the wounds into a win. Because He is good.

"He shall deliver you in six troubles, Yes, in seven no evil shall touch you. In famine He shall redeem you from death, And in war from the power of the sword. You shall be hidden from the scourge of the tongue, And you shall not be afraid of destruction when it comes" (Job 5.19–21).

Not one, two, or three troubles. And when you think God is at the end and says six troubles, He adds one more! And seven is the perfect number. Don't you wish one were the perfect number? One thing here. Remember that you will have trouble. But He will deliver you from every trouble one way or another with His presence in the process or a miracle instantaneously. Don't let the trials fool you. They are going to train you in righteousness.

"You shall know that your tent is in peace; You shall visit your dwelling and find nothing amiss. You shall also know that your descendants shall be many, And your offspring like the grass of the earth" (Job 5.24–25).

I love the emphasis upon the family in the book of Job. I also know that family is under attack in America. From legislation and government to culture and society, we have lost the biblical definition of family and are therefore losing the most important influence on the development of a society. We must get our society back to a healthy family foundation. Notice the peace and the longevity that is promised in the home. Young people need a healthy home. We can deal with anything when we have a healthy empire. Ultimately God will defend the family that trusts in Him and give that family a long life that is lived through their offspring.

"You shall come to the grave at a full age, As a sheaf of grain ripens in its season. Behold, this we have searched out; It is true. Hear it, and know for yourself" (Job 5.26–27). Finally, I love how God takes away the fear of death. This generation already feels invincible. Now God promises that our days will be full and that He alone calls our beginning and our end. Now that appears odd since so many have passed so quickly it seems. Remember that it is not how many days are in your life, but, how much life is in your days. Your days are defined by your dash.

The life you live between your birthdate and your death. For Jane, it was 1962 2015. And she won! Because she defined her dash. Our family learned a very important lesson in this season of our life. That if you win in life, you cannot lose in death!

Do not see the dash in your life as a number. See it as a value. The last verse in this great chapter says simply that these words are true. Count on them. Search and look for every reason for your suffering, but in the end, you will see that God is true and faithful.

Learning To Rethink
You can tell by your response to hardship what kind of person you are. Are you a fight or flight person? Have you been trained to contend or complain? Are you more willing to accept or reject the challenge? Is it easier

for you to play the game or to deflect the blame? We have to train our mind before the hardship comes. By doing that, we will use the trial for a triumph. We will put our chaos on His canvas. By training our mind, we can believe that our mess is His message. Without a strong mind, it is too easy to get pouty in the problems. Don't lose heart in the hardship. And don't be selfish in the suffering. Learn to unlearn old ways that are not helping you respond correctly to hardship.

As Solomon says often in Proverbs, "There is a way that seems right to a man, but, the end of this is death." We have too many things that we have learned in America that must be unlearned. It may seem right, but it is wrong to think that we don't deserve hardship. Or we are cursed if it comes to us. That is spoiled Western thinking. In the University of Suffering, we are taught to think differently. There is always a professor in the room who is smarter than we are or a rabbi who knows the way. And His thinking is the right way. Solomon was the wisest man to ever live. Think about that. What if Solomon were your professor? In some way, he really is. And His advice to us is simple. Our way of thinking is the wrong way. So we must listen to the rabbi.

One of the great preachers of all time was Charles Spurgeon. Early in his ministry, he went through a very trying experience that cost him great pain. While preaching to a crowd of over ten thousand, the building caught on fire. As a panic ensued, many people were injured as they exited the building. Along with the injured, seven people lost their lives that evening. People around Spurgeon said that he almost quit the ministry because of the guilt he carried from this crisis. The newspapers and many people in the community were hard on the young preacher because his preaching was so strong. His text that evening was a message on God's wrath upon the house.

Charles Spurgeon had to rethink. It was very difficult for him to recover. This moment in his life became unbearable. Imagine being a pastor, and while preaching to thousands of people, the building burns down, and thousands of people are put in a life-and-death situation. The reports from the story even said that two thousand people were outside the building who prevented the people inside from exiting. On top of that, the city and the media are now bearing down on you with the blame for this event. The people around Spurgeon, even his family, said he was going to quit the ministry because of this hardship. But in the lowest moment of his life, Spurgeon had a decision to make.

When Spurgeon ascended the pulpit on November 2, two weeks later, he opened with a prayer. "We are assembled here, O Lord, this day, with mingled feelings of joy and sorrow. Thy servant feared that he should never be able to meet this congregation again. But meet us with your grace oh God."

Although he would never fully recover from this disaster, Spurgeon's ministry did not end on that October day in 1856. He later said, "I have gone to the very bottoms of the mountains, as some of you know, in a night that never can be erased from my memory. But, as far as my witness goes, I can say that the Lord is able to save unto the uttermost and in the last extremity, and he has been a graceful God to me."

How did Spurgeon recover? It took several years, but his friends say that the joy he exhibited after this trial was heaven-sent grace. Spurgeon's joy was based not only on his own ability to recover but on God's ability to restore him with forgiveness. The pressure of the press and the negative things being said about him actually stirred London to greater attendance at his meetings. More people were hearing the gospel and responding because of the tragedy. And God used that fire as a formative moment, not only in Spurgeon's life but on the religious landscape of London itself. Many of the churches in the city banded together because of this tragedy. And everyone who knew Spurgeon said that what happened in his ministry as a result of this hardship afterward was miraculous. He went through the University of Suffering and graduated with a degree in maturity, overcoming the desire to quit the ministry because he did not allow hardship to defeat him. He had won the battle of the mind.

When I was in college, one of the things I learned was to write down the key principle or phrase that I learned in every class. I can go through many of my notebooks from university and see a main phrase for my classes. It was the main takeaway from every course. For instance, in psychology, one of the lessons I learned was that people are shaped by their most formative moments in life. In sociology, I learned that youth leaders should be the greatest sociologists on the planet. When I took homiletics, the statement, "Prepare your life before the sermon," moved me. In the same vein, let me give you the main phrases or key lessons learned in the courses I have taken as I went through hardship in the past two years.

Here is a bullet list of my most important courses that I passed before graduating from the University of Suffering:

- **Hardship 101—Introduction to Suffering**: The key to this course was understanding that suffering is universal to humanity.
- **Hardship 201—Rethinking Suffering**: Sometimes what we unlearn is as important as what we learn.
- **Hardship 301—Practicum in Suffering**: Even if we do not see it, there is always grace in every story.
- **Hardship 401—Theology of Suffering**: God doesn't keep us from hardship. He redeems hardship in our life for His purposes.

I felt really dumb in the beginning stages of my mess. Although I thought I had all of the right answers, many were to questions that were not that important. My education really took off when I admitted that suffering is universal. And I had to unlearn things that were getting in the way of me successfully maneuvering difficulty. While I was going through hardship in a practical way, it helped to know that God was my teacher, my rabbi.

See, my theology had to change. God never misses a moment. He doesn't miss an opportunity to redeem anything we are going through. Nothing in our life blindsides Him. And He will use all of it to confer upon each of us a degree in maturity from the University of Suffering.

Still to this day, the greatest lesson I have learned from a young person came from Kayla. If you knew her, you were taught some valuable lessons from her life. She had many surgeries on her leg to correct growth problems and persistent pain because of this. Her leg was deformed and looked differently from the other. It caused her to walk with a limp and to be in constant pain. But you never heard her complain. To be honest, I never knew her story in all of the years that I knew her. You want to know why?

It was almost unnoticeable. I mean, you knew it and couldn't help but to see it. But it wasn't a focal point of her relationships or her language. She just had settled this part of her life and dealt with it out of the public's eye. Kayla had a spiritual strength about her that made you see her grace and her beauty. She wouldn't even let you feel sorry for her. She is, by far, one of the most mature young believers I have ever met. And her troubled leg was always my second thought when I saw her. The first thought was how spiritually strong she was.

I mentored Kayla for a year. We talked about authority, spiritual gifts, ministry, intercession, and family. But we never dwelled on this condition of her leg or situation of hers.

#ifjobhadtwitter The University of Suffering is where we all can receive a degree in spiritual maturity if we are willing to graduate

Chapter 7
THE POWER OF EMOTIONAL QUOTIENT (EQ)

*The pain that you are feeling cannot be
compared to the joy that will be coming.*

—Apostle Paul

You will never be able to avoid the storms of life. But you will always be able to dance in the rain. Perspective is a great teacher. Being able to overcome hardship in life has much to do with our mentality. Instead of allowing the rain to house you, get out of the house and walk in the rain. We will never be able to control what happens to us. What we can control is how we respond to what happens to us. Balancing our emotions and training the mind is the key to overcoming circumstances. It is not about how much we know. It is more about how well we manage what we know.

There is a difference between intelligence quotient (IQ) and emotional quotient (EQ). Our IQ is the level of our knowledge of information and how we acquire and use it. Our EQ is how we process that information and how we respond to it. Too many people value the IQ above the EQ. As valuable as our IQ is to us, our emotions are just as important to our development as our intellect. The stability of our lives is dependent upon both. Hardship, like rain, will come to each of us. How we respond to it is critical. And that takes a lot of training.

The Snowflake Generation

There is a new term floating around that defines this generation as soft and fragile. The Snowflake generation is really not even a specific age range as much as it is a trait of anyone who fits the description. For example, a boomer-generation dad could be a snowflake if he is spoiled, acting elite, or being soft to criticism. But most of the snowflake reference is pointed at labeling the millennials, the Z's, the Y's, or the Like's (most sociological models haven't decided upon what to call this generation). They are the kids of the boomer parents who were spoiled by a culture that labeled them gifted and called them elite and special. They do not deal with hardship very well.

I saw this play out recently while in an airport. A twentysomething, who obviously was not doing well in college, was complaining to the gate agent that her flight was not going to get her home in time for class. She was upset with the agent and placing the blame for her situation solely on the airline. But, the main problem was that she didn't have any more skips. Seriously, it was quite a scene with raised voice, tears, and all. Of course, my first response was mercy. I love these kids. But then I realized she probably was not doing well in school because of her condition. She was fragile. The real problem was that she had already slept in too many times, and now the airline is at fault, along with the rest of us who were watching this drama. That is a perfect example of a snowflake.

A Disney Story

I have often said that the best kids do not always come from the best homes. Nor do the worst kids come from the worst homes. As a matter of fact, I have seen the worst kids come from the best homes and the best kids come from the worst homes. This is directly related to how we process the information in our lives. Setting is not always the dictator. Often it is not setting that dictates our response to hardship, but our EQ dictates our response to hardship.

Remember the young middle schooler who came up to me to pray for me? He was dealing with his own issues and placed all of that aside to pray for me, not even thinking about his situation. This is not a snowflake. This was a young teenager who put his situation aside to pray for my situation. If you ask me, he was operating with an extremely high EQ. His EQ was in high gear and handling everything that was coming his way. And he was controlling his response to hardship rather than hardship controlling his response to his situation.

A picture is being painted in America of a Disney generation who lives a story that includes a prince, a princess, a dragon, and an enchanted kiss at the end of every situation. This couldn't be further from reality because most of the palaces we live in are broken and the story does not always end with a kiss.

Immune From Hardship?
Hardship is going to come to each of us. So what will our attitude be? Here are two thoughts when hardship hits the palace: cause and effect.

Cause and Effect
God may not be the cause of our situation, but He will be there because of our situation. To see this before it comes to us will be the key to the battle. I recognize that, just because I am American or Christian, I am not immunized against suffering. It's because of this thing called free will, mine and other people.

Free will is a remarkable thing. It humanizes us when we are stupid. It humbles us when we start to think too highly of ourselves. Another thing about free will is that, when God gave us it, He took the pressure off from us of thinking that He is the cause of everything bad. For example, I could bang my head against a wall at my own choosing. That doesn't mean God is going to take away the pain or the *dain bramage*. There are many causes of hardship. Sometimes accidents happen. And other times we are the cause of them. Sometimes sickness happens. And other times we are even the cause of that. But although we believe that God can intervene and do miracles and the supernatural in the midst of these difficult times, we also believe that He can be present in these times and redeem accidents and sickness for His glory.

In relation to free will, we have the concept of cause and effect. I have always felt that, once we know the cause of our hardship, the better we are able to affect the effect. Stay with me now. The better able we are to control the outcome, the better we can prepare ourselves to deal with whatever has come our way and to affect the result. If we know the source (the cause) of the difficulty, it can be much easier to deal with suffering (the effect). This handling of trial can happen through our attitude or our action. Let me explain what I mean by that.

When I found out that Jane was diagnosed with cancer, I said immediately, "God, I know you can." My attitude was kicking in. But we also needed to get the right people around us too. And our actions kicked in by surrounding us with people who would play key roles in our family over the most difficult time in our lives. Our attitude and actions became vital in the battle against hardship. And your attitude and actions should prepare you to deal with your difficulties. I have shared some of those stories of the people who came alongside us in chapter 5. I can tell you that the people around me definitely shaped my EQ. Remember, don't do hardship alone.

The Cause Of Hardship

God may not be the cause of our hardship, but He is there because of it. We are not immune from hardship for several reasons, mostly because *we* are the cause of it, partly because *others* are the cause of it, and, in some cases, *God* is the cause of it. But we can be assured that, whatever the cause, God will be with us because of our situation. It is true that free will (our own and that of others) is the cause of most of the hardship that we face. And it is also true that God may be the cause of some of it. Understanding this can make hardship much easier to navigate. We know there is a purpose for it. And a person is in it with us.

God may not be the cause of my trouble but he is there because of my trouble.

Just because we live in America does not make us immune to difficulty. And just because God is love and He is good doesn't mean He will keep us from difficulty. On the contrary, God uses discipline or difficulty to shape us. Understanding this will help us to choose the better way of dealing with hardship: the way of betterment and not bitterness, the way of purpose and not pointless, and the way of agreement and not anger. In times of hardship, we sometimes need His presence and not an explanation.

Here are a couple of thoughts about our attitude and thinking when hardship hits the palace—first *our concept of God* and then *our concept of time*.

Our Concept Of God

We need to know that our EQ is one of the most important controllers in the midst of hardship. If our mind can trigger balance and assessment instead of imbalance and anger, we will manage crisis much better. Our mind must see God in the midst of our hardship, Our response to hardship most often depends upon our concept of God. We must see in scripture that God uses hardship and difficulty for many reasons, whether to bring glory to His name, to get our or others' attention, or even to step in when hardship happens in our life outside of His doing. That's a thought now, huh? When things happen, we often look for a reason. Maybe the reason is simply that life happens. And God had nothing to do with the happening. But He wants to have everything to do with the process and the outcome. God did not send that something that comes into our life.

Upon seeing this, He will then step in and be with us in the matter. So we need to know that we will experience free will, ours and others'. But God will mix His will into the matter also.

East and West Thinking
What we must understand is that God and Christianity see hardship from a completely different angle than our culture in the West. The Eastern culture is comfortable with suffering. Christianity embraces hardship as a tutor to greater character and ultimately blessings. But the Western mind-set says that hardship comes to those who are weak or deserve punishment. And hardship is an evil and must be avoided. And this Western mind-set is painting a picture in America of a Disney generation who lives a storybook life that includes a prince, a princess, a dragon, and an enchanted kiss at the end of every story. This couldn't be further from reality. Most of the palaces we live in are broken. And the story of hardship, suffering, and pain does not always end in the form of an affectionate kiss.

We should take our concept of God from the scriptures and not culture. Reading through the Bible is a lesson on who God is and how He uses hardship to shape someone. Reading through culture is a lesson on who God is not and how He uses hardship to punish someone. The countless stories of people overcoming hardship with the purposes and presence of God are the model we must follow when hardship hits our life. If we have proven anything in this book, it is that God thinks differently from our world about hardship. And we must get His mind on the matters of suffering if we are going to navigate suffering with success. When hardship hits the palace of our lives, our concept of God's purposes and His presence in suffering will be the mind-set we want to have to come out on the other end as a king or a queen.

Our Concept Of Time
Our concept of time also determines our response to hardship. One of the most helpful verses to me in the New Testament is in 1 Corinthians 13.12

where Paul said of suffering and inequity, "I see through a glass dimly, but then, face to face." He was giving us perspective to help us through difficulty, that is, the perspective of time and understanding the frailty of life on earth through minds that cannot comprehend the purposes of God. I love the words "but then." It leads us to the future hope. Time is hopeful. And when time is filled with hope and not despair, time is even more powerful.

Hope Dealers

We are all *hope dealers* in a sense, a term I saw a youth ministry and an inner -city Church use as a series on the power of hope. It fits perfectly with this idea of *my broken palace*, the concept of balanced thinking. We often portray our lives as perfect castles and ornate palaces, as gardens and not jungles, without corruption or blemish, when, in reality, we are really broken. I see it all the time in America. A machismo that says, "I'm okay; you're okay." Pop psychology that cannot deal with the reality of the wave of suffering in our lives.

My broken palace speaks of the power of hope. Through stories of teens whose lives were torn apart by hardship, hope was the answer they needed to cope. We must all be hope dealers to a generation who is buried by despair. Hope is something I have used countless times in my ministry to young people. Teenagers are growing up in a world that is defined by suicide, self-harm, broken families, the sexual revolution, out-of-control social media, our post-Christian society, and the Coexist movement. As adults and youth leaders, we must bring the balance and the maturity to a teen's life while he or she is in the midst of a broken world falling apart around them.

When I speak with a suicidal teen boy, I draw him to hope by extending his life and telling him I'll talk with him tomorrow. When I speak with a young girl who is cutting and doing self-harm, I draw her to hope by saying she is not the only one going through this. When I speak with a teenage boy who is living with a grandparent because divorce is tearing apart his home, I model to him my family or another youth leader's home so he can see there is hope for him to stop the dysfunction. By dealing hope we can get people to focus upon the answer and not the problem.

Emotional Quotient (EQ)

Over and over, hope becomes the anchor in a sea of despair. It becomes the EQ that holds someone together and stabilizes every bit of information that is coming into our lives. Our concept of time is really hope. And hope is patience. Patience will place us in a powerful position of perspective. Where there is hope, there is always a way.

Our emotional strength is a lifesaver. It manages crisis and files data with balance and not emotional highs and lows. Here are two ways to develop EQ if you are going through a difficult time right now.

1. *Slow Down Crisis*
Be careful of reacting too quickly to hardship. Take a spiritual count-to-ten. Then measure the data and situation with facts and not fear, worry, or ignorance. Slowing down crisis can actually reduce the stress.

2. *Debrief after Crisis*
Often after a crisis, we realize it wasn't as bad as we thought, right? Think about the last time you freaked out about something. It probably wasn't worth all of the emotion and reaction. Am I right? Taking time to evaluate and assess a hardship after it passes can help us to deal with the next one when it comes more effectively.

> *We have become buried under the social tsunami of suicide, self-harm, broken families, the sexual revolution, an out-of-control social media, our post-Christian society, and the Coexist movement. And too often we cannot even think because of the pressure.*

> *But hope has become the message of salvation to a society that is inundated by the pressure of these things.*

Be a *hope dealer* in our culture today for people who think they have no hope. Fill time with hope and not with despair or worry. And everyone around you will buy what you are selling.

The Snowflake Generation

Snowflake is one of the new terms for our generation. You know, soft or fleeting. Or if you lack constancy or have no constitution. Or if you need safe places on the university campus or are afraid of the language of trauma. Or if you are thinking critically and not doing critical thinking. It is the part of the reason that 70 percent of us are unhappy with our country (CNBC). We have created a panacea of perfection that will not allow for hardship. So when it comes, we become incoherent and unable to cope. Maybe we should turn off one of our flat-screens, take a week off from social media, and thank our boss for our job. This isn't a new problem.

A few years ago, *The David Letterman Show* identified the present American attitude toward life. The popular talk-show host began his late-night show with the following words on America and our attitudes:

> *As most of you know I am not a President Bush fan. Nor have I ever been, but this is not about Bush. It is about us as Americans, and it seems to hit the mark. Maybe you hear how bad the president is on the news or a talk show. Did this news affect you so much, make you so unhappy you couldn't take a look around for yourself, and see all the good things and be glad? Think about it. Are you upset at the president because he actually caused you personal pain?*

His comments were in relation to the *Newsweek* magazine article and poll that alleged about 67 to 71 percent of Americans were unhappy with the direction the country was headed and the state of the United States in

2008. In essence, the article was saying that two-thirds of the country is negative about the condition of our country and they want a change.

Here we are almost a decade later. And the same thoughts are being replayed today in America repeatedly on all media outlets. But with just another President and a new set of problems.

This all made me think about what we have here in America. No, our country isn't perfect. But maybe we need a little perspective. Letterman went on to ask the question, "What are we so unhappy about?"

- *Is our unhappiness that we have electricity and running water twenty-four hours a day, seven days a week?*
- *Is our unhappiness the result of having air-conditioning in the summer and heating in the winter?*
- *Could it be that 95.4 percent of these unhappy folks have a job?*
- *Maybe it is the ability to walk into a grocery store and see more food than Darfur has seen in the last year?*
- *Maybe our unhappiness is because of our ability to drive our cars from the Pacific Ocean to the Atlantic Ocean without having to present identification papers as we move through each state?*
- *Or possibly the hundreds of clean and safe motels we would find along the way that provide temporary shelter?*
- *I guess having thousands of restaurants with varying cuisine from around the world is just not good enough either as we drive across the country in our vehicles?*
- *Or could it be that we are unhappy because, when we wreck our car, emergency workers show up and provide services to help all and even send a helicopter to take you to the hospital if you need it?*
- *Perhaps you are unhappy because you are one of the 70 percent of Americans who own a home?*
- *You may be upset with knowing that, in the unfortunate case of a fire, a group of trained firefighters will appear in moments and use top-notch*

equipment to extinguish the flames, thus saving you, your family, and your belongings?

- *Or if, while at home watching one of your many flat-screen TVs, a burglar or prowler intrudes, an officer equipped with a gun and a bulletproof vest will come to defend you and your family against attack or loss?*

- *Could it be that we are unhappy with a few things but forget that we live in a neighborhood free of bombs or militias raping and pillaging the residents? Neighborhoods where 90 percent of teenagers own cell phones, computers, or cars?*

- *Or are we unhappy because of the complete religious, social, and political freedoms we enjoy that are the envy of the world?*

Reading this article on Letterman got me thinking. Is this what has almost 70 percent of people today in America unhappy? Gratefulness would go a long way. It changes perspective. Is the glass half full or half empty? I think that all depends on what is in the glass. Instead of critical thinking, we are thinking critical. There's a big difference. Have we become more critical than we are thinking?

Letterman gave quite a lengthy sermon from a much larger pulpit than most ministers have in America. And this homily is a much-needed message for America.

Maybe we have lost our gratitude and willingness to focus upon the beauty around us. Maybe our perspective needs to change. Letterman completes the rant with these closing thoughts,

Fact is, we are the largest group of ungrateful, spoiled brats the world has ever seen. No wonder the world loves the U.S., yet has a great disdain for its citizens. They see us for what we are—the most blessed people in the world who do nothing but complain about what we don't have and what we hate about the country instead of thanking the good Lord we live here.

Are we spoiled? Are we unable to think positively? Where are the principles that guide us? Where is our constitution? I'm not asking that we turn the other cheek and settle for mediocrity. I am not asking that we build a Pollyanna facade of a nation that isn't willing to look deep into our hearts to find injustice and to rid ourselves of it. I know we are living in the face of hurricanes, earthquakes, tornadoes, fires, racial injustice, and moral declination. But to also see the blessings that surround us should change our focus upon the kindness around us also.

In hardship, time is a teacher, and understanding is a healer. For now, we see through a glass dimly but then face-to-face. So hang on. You may not know why now. But then again, when you get there, you may not need to know. I've learned one thing through these past years of hardship. If things are bad, they are not over. In the end, God will make all things good. So if they are not good, it's not the end. Patience will see you to the end, where you will finally see clearly.

I was speaking at public high school to a packed gymnasium. As usual, when I was done, students like to talk. I think sometimes they like to talk because they can stay out of class a little longer! But waiting in the line was a young girl who was standing with the principal. As the line came to an end, the principal introduced me to her and said she needed to talk with me. So we went back to the principal's office, and he let me use the office while he sat outside the window.

As we began talking, she couldn't look at me. She was definitely an alternative-type kid and was dressed in all black and with jet-black hair that covered her face. I tried to get her to talk, but she was not exactly in the mood. After a few moments, she let me in by stating that she wanted to kill herself. So I replied to her, "No, you don't."

That got her attention. As she looked up at me flipping mad, she replied matter-of-fact that she really did want to kill herself. And then she asked me why I told her that she didn't want to. I simply replied to her in as loving a way that I could "If you really wanted to kill yourself, you wouldn't have told me. You would have just done it. But I think you wanted me to know." She started to cry.

I was relieved that it worked! After she told me the rest of the story, we spent about ten minutes talking and putting a plan together to speak with a counselor and to change a few things in her life. The principal walked back into the room to a completely different young lady.

Man, was I glad that worked. I have never used that tactic before or since with a suicidal person. And I wouldn't recommend it.

#ifjobhadtwitter Sometimes I do not control my situation or the outcome. But always I control my attitude in the midst of it.

Chapter 8
TIME DOESN'T HEAL

*Remember that we were created in the image of
God. And that reality means that we are created
in both His blessing and His suffering.*

—Ravi Zacharias

During the writing of this book, my daughter Jorie and I were talking one day. While we were talking, she said to me, "Daddy, God told me that the pain doesn't get easier. But His grace gets stronger." We were talking about how the healing process gets easier over time. Not easy, but easier. We talked about how time doesn't heal. Time is just hours, days, weeks, months, and years. But what we do with our time heals. We have to give time something to work with. I believe that we all give time something to work with. If we give time our despair, it will yield depression and heaviness. If we give time our doubt, it will yield questions and confusion. If we give time our fear, it will yield anxiety and stress. If we give time our anger, it will yield self-harm. But if we give time our faith, it will yield grace.

Wow, what a revealing moment of wisdom for me when Jorie introduced the growth of grace into this writing. I had already seen it operating in our family. I guess it really just took my daughter revealing what she was doing with her time as she was healing from the loss of her mother. The growth of grace is an amazing thought. That grace can be as simple or as complex as our problems. That grace can be as gentle or as powerful as we need it to be. That grace could increase with the degree of my suffering. We know there is grace for our salvation and the forgiveness of sins, but grace also becomes very real in suffering. It becomes sufficient in suffering and comparable in chaos. Grace manifests in the mess. And in our hardship, grace is the harbor from the storms raging around us. My children taught me many things from their own experiences.

I've heard people say that experience is the greatest teacher. I cannot give you a quantitative analysis of whether books, professors, or degrees are greater instructors than experience. But I can give you very real anecdotal proof that, in our family's case, experience was deep at work in the healing process. In the most difficult days of their lives, each of my kids was filling my time with everything I needed for healing. And much of that did not come from their education.

I would like to say that I was holding up my kids at this time, but each of them in his or her own way has played a vital role in my healing. Every time we would talk to each other, we asked the same question.

We would say, "How are you?"

And the same confident reply came back. "I'm doing fine if you are. I'm only concerned about you. If you are good, then I am good."

It became great comfort to know that we were each supporting the other. To be completely honest, we must all have been hoping that the other was doing better than we actually were! If you are in a hardship now, keep the family close, speak honestly with them, be sure to hold and kiss each other, and look each other in the eyes when you talk. The eyes say something.

What Can You Bring To Crisis?

My oldest son Jaren, his wife Kristin, and our grandson Maddox were just leaving for L.A. and would go through the first months of our new reality without the immediate family to process everything with. It certainly helped that my youngest brother Ric and his partner Matt were in L.A. They had come up to Minneapolis and spent several weeks with us the last month of Jane's life. So they understood everything we were all going through.

One of the things that Ric and Matt have taught all of us is how important family is. They were managing their companies and flying to multiple cities for a month during the whole process of Jane's last month. As our family would visit, they placed everyone in the hotel across the street from us in downtown Minneapolis and brought groceries and plenty of Chinese food! What can you offer your family when you go through hardship? What is your family offering you in your hardship?

Time deserves our family. And the family deserves time. Family time is the support system that every person needs in a time of blessing or in a time of suffering. The support system is needed in life and death. Unfortunately, in America, the family has been disintegrated and, in most cases, lacks the integrity to be present in times of crisis. The family should be the place where all of us can navigate the good and the bad. The family should be the place where we can be ourselves and find the help we need in times of blessing and suffering. The family should be a deterrent to many of the things that are destroying people today. Remember, the family is the one unit that exists in every sector of society—government, education, entertainment, and the urban, suburban, and rural settings. The family is global. And family will always be there in blessing and suffering. That is why it is so important for the family to be healthy.

Ric and Matt modeled to us how important family really is. I think we already knew it but it became even more apparent. We must give the family time in order for our nation to be rebuilt. Family must be at the center of it all. As the one unit that exists in every continent, nation, state, city, and neighborhood, I believe humankind rises and falls on the strength and the weakness of family. That is why it is so important for family to be part of your time. You can be assured that healing will be much easier and complete in a healthy family. Keep the family healthy, and you will be able to navigate through anything life throws your way.

Raised At The Altar And The Gym

Jane loved the principle of sowing and reaping. I think it showed in how we raised our kids. We raised our kids at the altar and the gym. We spent a lot of time at both of these locations. I am so glad we took the time in our family to raise our kids with the discipline of the scriptures with prayer and in the church. And I am so glad that we taught them the discipline of athletics, teamwork, and the gym! That was time well spent.

Our kids knew that there were a few very important sectors in our lives: the family, the church, the school, the community, and the team. Each of these was contributors to the kind of kids we raised. After all, it does take a village to raise our kids. And our philosophy was that our kids were going to help raise our village where we lived.

Jane used to talk about sowing and reaping all the time. In the final month of Jane's battle, each of our kids had a huge impact on our situation, but only because we had taken the time to sow into our kid's lives for twenty-five years. So in the most important time of our lives, as parents, we would reap everything we had sown into their lives.

During the last month or so of our battle, Jaren, Kristin, and Maddox moved in with us several times to help. Watching Jaren lead the family was inspiring to me. Because I spent almost every hour with Jane, he and Kristin were great to have around, especially with the grandson running around. Literally Maddox brought so much life into our lives. I would often wonder going through this battle of how people who are alone and have no support system would deal with hardship.

At the opening of the book, we challenged you to deal with hardship the right way, to be adopted into the family of Christianity, not the family of anger, the family of doubt, or the family of alcohol. And we also address the idea of community and the crew around us in another chapter. That we should not go through hardship alone. Hearing the activity, conversations, laughter, and prayers of a strong family is great comfort in our story. Even though we were going through the most difficult time of our lives, somehow it seemed bearable and hopeful because we were together. I want you to hear from each of my kids.

Jaren Speaking Now
The human reaction to anything when things don't add up or don't go your way is to immediately lose hope. You don't get that job, or you feel inadequate or unwanted. Your finances have been struggling, or you feel hopeless and incapable. For me, my mom got sick, and I felt lost and unsteady. My entire world was suddenly thrust into the unknown. The most important central figure in my life was my mother. She was my everything, my rock. And to hear the word "cancer" was something I was not prepared for.

God has been consistently teaching me about trust. It's relatively easy to talk about trust. It's completely different to follow through with it when hard times hit. When you stand on top of a table and fall back into a group of people ready to catch you (trust falls are the worst, by the way), you trust they will indeed catch you. I found myself trusting and believing that God still had my back as I was falling, that He still cared for me. And in 1 Peter 5.7, it says we can actually place all of our anxieties on Him because He cares for us.

As I watched Jaren lead, it was interesting to me. He is a man of few words and yet commands such great respect. I'm not sure I've met a more humble person in my life with so many gifts.

Jorie Speaking Now

I've learned to live life more carefree, enjoying each day as it comes and living in the moment. I have counted my time more valuable than before. It's made me more heaven and kingdom minded, seeing beyond my little circle or circumstances. Today, after the death of my mom, I see the bigger picture and not just what happens to me any given day.

One of the things I have learned is that trusting God is the best and only thing you can do sometimes. When the pain, trial, difficulty, or heartache comes at you, all you can do sometimes is to simply trust that the Holy Spirit will give you what you need in that moment.

That's what it gets down to for me, moments. And God's presence is in every moment. Whether it is comfort, joy, peace, maybe a friend, or even wisdom from God, along the way you will learn what it looks like to trust in Him. As you trust Him, you see the true and unique faithfulness of God! Losing my mom was the hardest thing I went through. But His grace gets stronger with the pain. God has never let me down, and I know He never will.

Listening to Jorie makes me so glad we took the time early in our family for faith formation. I wish you knew my children like I do. When I think back at the time we spent getting ready for church, having family devotion at the dinner table, involving the family in youth ministry, and praying over our kids in their rooms, I can see the outcomes. Can you feel it in the words of my kids? Believe me, this isn't just content for a book on hardship, suffering, and trial. I get this all the time from my kids.

Justen Talking Now

There is nothing we can't handle. Nothing. No matter how bad it gets. Our family has seen a lot lately. But we're not alone. I was quiet and shocked going through this at first, and I didn't want to talk. But my friends stepped up and made me. When I understood how important it was to open up, I was fine. Realizing that my friends were an important part of my healing changed everything. Don't think that you can handle crisis and hardship on your own. You can handle anything. Just not alone. When you don't want to talk about it you need to get the right people around you to help you discuss it.

Did you hear that? Wow! Justen is our youngest, and he is with me. Jaren and Jorie are married and would have someone to process everything with. Because Justen was with me, we would process everything together. We would watch each other go through this battle and learn from each other. He would soon become a rock for me with his attitude, honesty, and strength. Justen has never lacked honesty in his life. It is one of his greatest traits. He doesn't fake anything. And his openness in this season helped me to see that he was dealing with it properly. And he challenged me to do the same.

You have heard it said before. What most reveals our character is difficulty. It's easy to contend and win when things are going well and when we are in the blessing. But who are we, and how do we respond when things are not going well when we are in the suffering? As Christians, we must be mature enough to accept both blessing and suffering and see the value in responding with courage.

Time will tell our response only if we give time the proper thing to work with. What we are investing in the time of our crisis will be the fruit of the season after our crisis is over. We will reap what we sow. I think we need some realism in our fantasy gap. Since hardship and trial are part of Christianity and scripture, why are we so upset that they are in Christians and culture?

Read again what Ravi Zacharias said in the quote at the beginning of this chapter. "Remember that we were created in the image of God. And that reality means that we are created in both His blessing and His suffering." There is so much we need to unlearn in life, especially for those of us in America and especially as it relates to hardship. Let me give you five quick things that we should give time when we have gone through a crisis:

1. **Honesty:** Don't be afraid to call your situation what it is. You cannot avoid the facts. From the beginning, face the truth. The only way you can do everything in your power is to know how severe or simple your situation is. Don't be afraid of asking questions and getting clarity about whatever you are going through. Ask questions and get second opinions. Whether you are dealing with sickness, debt, rumors, or relationship issues, get to the facts.

2. **Community:** Time will deal very well with crisis if you include friendships. This is dealt with specifically in chapter 5. When you have others walking through crisis with you, there is great wisdom and perspective in that kind of university, in that kind of gathering of minds and experiences. Community brings an education that you cannot bring to the situation by yourself.

3. **Hope:** Hope is like a calendar. We know the weekend is coming, and the closer it is to Friday, the more excited we get. No matter how desperate your situation is, there is always hope. Hope is really built on truth, not on a fantasy. Hope is like a drug. It is capable of changing our moods, our energy, and our attitude. When you get good news, how does it make you feel? Apply that daily to your situation, and you will build strength for each day. After all, we are all hope dealers!

4. **Persistence:** Get up every morning and breathe. And do it again tomorrow. The only time you will lose to anything is when you quit. Rah-rah-rah, I know. That sounds like positivity and cheerleading. But it is true. You have to be satisfied when you look in the mirror at yourself that you gave crisis everything you had with no regrets. When you are persistent, you don't get buried in the

moment. You live another hour, another day, another week, and another month.

5. **Faith:** This is the spiritual assurance that you are not alone in your situation. What God says in His Word is true. What does this look like? Speak to the circumstances of your life with confidence that, even though you cannot see the evidence of God working, He is working still the same. But you may have to adjust how you think God is going to work. Think of the many times you have seen God do something in your life. And apply the faith that He can and will do it again. Speak faith every morning, afternoon, and evening, and do not speak doubt.

It's not like God is shielding us from hardship, suffering, and pain. He knows we need it. But a poor attitude in it has a lot to do with how long we stay in it. Sometimes God is simply trying to teach us something through hardship. And the quicker we learn, the faster the suffering passes. His grace becomes stronger in the moments during or after hardship. Grace works around the clock.

In God's conversation with Job, He didn't place any time restraints on Satan's attacks. He didn't assure Job that "this will only take a few days." But God did give Satan a limit, that is, how much Satan could do in Job's life. That is a great reminder of how God works. No matter how long we have to go through something, He will not give us too much without a way of escape. And He will be with us in it.

If we are going to take the beauty from God and Christianity, we should then take the struggle. God did after all give us patience as one of the fruits of the Spirit. And patience is a time mover and a clock manager. It moves us to God and His help. Hardship should drive us to Christ. In Luke 2.8, even in the midst of fear, loneliness, oppression, hopelessness, and darkness, the story of Christ was good news. In the shadows, a light has come. Jesus is the light of the world, a city on a hill, the deliverer to oppressed, a friend of sinners, and the peace that surpasses our own think-ing. And even today, the gospel is still good news!

> *The FAITH of the church is for the FEARS of the world. Everything that this world needs can be found in the church. The one place and the one source for everything the world needs. We must learn to be as excited about being the church then we are about going to church. Remember the children's song years ago? This little light of mine, I'm going to let it shine!*

Christianity is the answer to everything in the world, the only message that comes from outside of the world and its resources. Our hope does not come from a place without it. It comes from the source of hope. If you are stuck in a cycle of looking and seeking for help in the wrong place, you will never find hope. You have to find the answer in the right place. And that place is Jesus.

Here is a look at some texts from the apostle Paul and his unique perspec-tive on hardship, suffering, and pain. As the central figure of the New Testament, he too, like Job, went through massive difficulties. His list of sufferings include, as stated in 2 Corinthians 6.38-39,

> hard labor, imprisonments, beatings, in frequent danger of death, five times received 39 lashes, three times beaten with rods, once stoned, three times shipwrecked, spent a night and a day in the open sea, in danger from rivers and from bandits, in danger from countrymen and from the Gentiles, in danger in the city and in the country, in danger on the sea and among false brothers, in labor and toil and often without sleep, in hunger and thirst and often without food, in cold and exposure.

And then Paul said that, apart from these external trials, he faced the daily pressure of his concern for all the church. Did you catch that? He was not as concerned about hardship as he was the church. I think we could all learn from his perspective on suffering. Listen to Paul for a few minutes and his perspective on hardship.

2 Corinthians 12.8–10 says, "Three times I pleaded with the Lord to take away the thorn in my flesh from me. But He said to me, 'My grace is sufficient for you, for My power is perfected in weakness.' Therefore, I will boast all the more gladly in my weaknesses, so that the power of Christ may rest on me. That is why, for the sake of Christ, I delight in weaknesses, in insults, in hardships, in persecutions, in difficulties. For when I am weak, then I am strong."

What a viewpoint of hardship. Paul was saying he would rather have God and His grace than to be whole and not have Him. And Paul was stating that the greatest concern for him was not the physical or social hardship. But the concern and the pressure was upon him to take care of the church. How many of us can say that the concern for the church in our life far outweighs our concern for the physical and economic or relational and social pressure we are under?

So you think you have it bad? Maybe a thorough look at the condition of the world will give you a different perspective. I mean, how many of us really have it that bad? Like I said at the beginning of the book, I am not the poster child for suffering. As most of you reading this book as well.

Our culture and scripture clearly include the concept of hardship in America. So there should be no surprises. But Paul writes about difficulty in the New Testament into perspective. In 2 Corinthians 1, Paul comforts those who are in difficulty and trials by offsetting the ever-present reality of suffering with the supernatural comfort of the Father.

"Blessed be the God and Father of our Lord Jesus Christ, the Father of mercies and God of all comfort, who comforts us in all our tribulation, that we may be able to comfort those who are in any trouble, with the comfort with which we ourselves are comforted by God."

And Solomon puts difficulty in the Old Testament into perspective. In Ecclesiastes 3.1 and 11, Solomon says that everything has a season, from birth and death, to mourning and dancing, and to war and peace. And Solomon says that everything is beautiful in its time, a powerful reminder to redeem hardship.

To everything there is a season, and a time for every purpose under heaven; a time to be born, a time to die…a time to kill, and a time to heal…a time to weep and a time to laugh, a time to mourn and a time to dance…a time of war and a time of peace. He has made everything beautiful in its time.

In these texts, I want you to simply count how many times the concept of suffering appears as opposed to how many times mercy appears. Suffering is defined with words like tribulation, trouble, and affliction. These words occur about six times in the first text. Almost overwhelming, isn't it? But look at the way Paul counters the existence of suffering. He uses words such as mercy, comfort, consolation, salvation, hope, and steadfast. These words occur about fifteen times. I think there is an emphasis we are to take notice of.

For as the sufferings of Christ abound in us, so our consolation also abounds through Christ. Now if we are afflicted, it is for your consolation and salvation, which is effective for enduring the same sufferings which we also suffer. Or if we are comforted, it is for your consolation and salvation. And our hope for you is steadfast, because we know that as you are partakers of the sufferings, so also you will partake of the consolation.

And look at the counterbalance in Ecclesiastes. For every hardship, there is an answer. I want you to see that hardship is a reality. That suffering is apparent. But you can count on the supernatural presence of God to bring consolation. The purposes of heaven are not delayed or forgotten. God is more focused upon comforting you than allowing suffering in your life. We just need to keep in mind that there is a season for everything. That includes hardship. People ask me all the time why I am still in youth ministry after thirty-four years. I often give several reasons. I think this is a time issue and many leaders do not value longevity. There are many reasons why I'm still doing this, but here are a few.

First, God called me to do this. I talk with Him every day, and He hasn't asked me to do anything else.

Second, I told God, when I stop crying for teenagers, I would get out. I still haven't stopped crying for teenagers.

Third, I would rather help teens write their stories than to listen to adults tell theirs.

Fourth, everything is failing and changing (the family and the world) around teenagers. I want to be there. And youth leaders should desire to be there so we can be someone they can trust and know with certainty that we will always be there.

I used the same kind of commitment to youth ministry as I did in this trial we went through. I was in it for the long haul. You need to let hardship, suffering, and trial know that you are in it and will not quit. We must see the importance of time in everything. Get a thirty-thousand foot view of your situation. Do not get buried in the moment- but get the whole picture. While you are going through hardship, suffering, and pain, embrace time as your friend. But remember that time doesn't heal. What we do with our time is what brings healing.

In the past year, numerous students have approached me with stories of parents or loved ones who have died. But in Massachusetts recently, a young girl came up to me and wanted to talk. I asked her name and then wanted to hear her story. She hesitated but began to tell me her story. Her mom had cancer and was not able to be involved in her life much. At the age of fourteen, this middle-school girl had to care for her mom, raise the younger siblings, put her volleyball aspirations on hold, and take care of the home. But she really didn't come up to me to talk about her situation.

So after quickly telling her story, she asked how I was doing. She wanted to encourage me. In the midst of everything she was going through, she wasn't thinking about herself and her situation. She was thinking about my loss and my situation. Hardship and suffering have a way of making us more concerned about others than we are about ourselves. She was laying a foundation as a young teen that would help her deal with any situation she would face in the coming years. And she was giving time what it needed to heal her in her situation.

#ifjobhadtwitter When it comes to hardship, it is not time that heals. When it comes to hardship, it is what we do with our time that heals.

Chapter 9
IS THIS REAL LIFE?

*I believe that suffering is really ignorance borne
from not understanding the purpose of pain.*

Dalai Lama

Reconciling Our Stories

On July 23, 2014, our day went from the highest of highs to the lowest of lows. You can't get any higher in life than to be parents at an only daughter's wedding. It was beautiful. We were having a blast enjoying the culmination of months of work, talking with family and friends, and watching our only daughter create the greatest memory of her life. The whole family was there. And we went from the ceremony of a lifetime to the dance floor. It was epic.

And then it happened. Throughout the day of the wedding, Jane began to develop bruises and became unusually tired. By the end of the day, she had around twenty to twenty-five bruises all over her body. Jane tried to cover it up and let everyone know that she was fine. Being the good husband that I am, I encouraged her that it was only exhaustion, and if the bruising persisted through the weekend, we would go to the doctor on Monday. I'm not sure those words really helped. Even so, the bruising persisted and worsened as we closed out the wedding and began to clean up Saturday evening.

We kissed our daughter and son-in-law good-bye and worked another hour until almost everyone was gone on his or her way. With just a few family members and close friends left who were cleaning and putting things away, I noticed Jane sitting down with a worried look on her face. We talked for a few minutes, and I could tell that something wasn't right. But because it was late, we decided to just go home and see how she felt in the morning, and if we needed to, we would go to the hospital then. We were blessed to have my brother's wife there with us that weekend. Kerri, a nurse, came over and began to speak to us. She looked at Jane as we were talking and firmly said that we should go to the emergency department (ED) immediately.

So dressed in our formal wear, we got into the Jeep and went to the ED while the family cleaned up the rest of the evening. To be honest, it felt like the right thing to do, and it gave us comfort to know that we wouldn't have to worry about anything. We arrived at the hospital, and after about four hours of testing and in the middle of the morning on Sunday, Jane was given a room for further observation.

The on-call doctor that night was a hematoma specialist. He was not supposed to be working the ED and actually told us he had only been in the ED by chance that night. But as we have found out, God was playing chess that evening. This man noticed what was going on immediately and alerted a team of physicians who were in our room by Sunday morning.

Jane was showing signs of a deficiency in coagulation (DIC), a rare blood disorder. That Sunday afternoon, another doctor came to our room and told us that he was pretty sure that, along with the DIC, Jane had a form of leukemia. I respectfully questioned him and pressed for more answers and a second opinion. He affirmed us that, going forward, everything would be thoroughly researched and her setting would be evaluated.

You can imagine what was going through our mind when he left our room. I was still dressed in my formal wear from the wedding, and with her formal wear hanging in the hospital room closet, Jane was placed in a hospital gown and admitted. She spent the next sixteen days in the hospital. About eight of those days were spent in ICU as we began to think through our next steps to take with this diagnosis.

Exhausted, we talked, prayed, and waited through the evening on Sunday and into the morning on Monday. Then a new team of doctors came to our room and introduced themselves to us. The first doctor, somewhat matter-of-fact, said to us that they wished Jane had leukemia. When he said those words, I shook my head slowly and thought, *Did he just say that?*

Instead he told us that Jane had stage four malignant metastatic melanoma, for which there was no cure outside of a miracle. It was like going from bad news to worse.

Jane Speaks

The following words in this book are from Jane and her journal. Here is Jane on her situation in her words.

Melanoma? That is a skin disease. I had no lesions, raised moles, or skin discoloration. Melanoma? How could I have melanoma? *If you ever met Jane, she was fair-skinned, and she rarely sat in the sun or tanned.* And what about stage one, two, or three? We had more testing done for the next forty-eight hours after the wedding, and after further tests, it was diagnosed that my setting began in the blood marrow and not the skin or a lesion. This is totally rare. Melanoma in the bloodstream and bone marrow? In fact, that 71 percent of my bone marrow was melanoma. And with that percentage and the numbers of my setting, there would be no chance of a bone marrow transplant. But things got even worse the next twenty-four hours as I was moved to ICU, fighting for my life for the next sixteen days with a bleeding problem. One day I began to bleed out, and my bed was soaked in blood. Immediately there were about five or six doctors and nurses in my room, and they were saving my life, working to stop the bleeding.

Aside from the melanoma, the DIC (deficiency in coagulation) was the most severe condition at the moment and could take my life quickly if I bled out. That is what was causing the bruises on my body all day on Saturday and Sunday. The doctor's biggest concern was that my blood was not clotting and that I could develop internal bleeding. One doctor told my husband in the hallway outside of the room that night that he didn't know if I would see Christmas and gave me just months to live. And that meant possibly missing the birth of our first grandson, due on December 15. I determined in my mind that nothing would make me miss Christmas or our first grandson's birth.

In just a few short days, we went from the highest of highs to the lowest of lows. And our life was turned upside down. And we were about to be tested as we never had been before. And looking back on all of this, we were ready. So prepared. Prepared by the word that Jeff received that morning from the Lord only two weeks before this about having no gods before Him. Prepared by that word to not even place our family before Him. That word prepared us for the faithfulness and the steady dedication of our lives to Christ that we would need to fight this diagnosis.

Is This Real Life?

Have you ever had a bad day? It was the perfect storm. It was incurable and unusual. We were told that the doctors and our team had only seen a few cases like ours in the United States, and they were talking to specialists across the country who were watching our case. Portland, Dallas, and Columbus cancer centers were all consulted. How could we be going through this right now? This week? We had the greatest life, marriage, family, and ministry. We ate healthy. I remember sitting in the hospital that first week in ICU curled up in a ball and looking at Jeff and saying, "Is this real life?" When I said that to him, I saw a strength in his eyes that I knew would carry us through this. That somehow I knew we could do this together.

Jeff would be at the hospital continuously. He would go home for a few hours and then ride his bike back up to the hospital and serve me. I remember thinking that this was what we vowed when we were married. That in sickness and health we would love each other. And even though we would never talk about end-of-life discussions through this whole next year in our life, the other part of our vows would be in the back of my mind. Until death do us part.

After telling our family, our pastors, and a few close friends, we made a statement on our social media and enlisted everyone to pray. And then in the midst of this, after about ten days in the hospital and over seventy blood transfusions, along with thousands of people praying, I began to make a turn for the better. My blood levels improved. Energy came back. The doctors would come in my room and look at me funny as I was sitting up in bed and say, "This is remarkable" or "amazing" or "We didn't expect this." The critical disorder in my blood, the DIC, was being reversed so quickly, and my energy and vitality was coming back. I would sit up in my room, greet the doctors or nurses with a smile, and tell them that God was healing me.

Finally, after sixteen days, we went home. The blood disorder was healed. And we began the fight against the cancer. Many men and women of God prayed for me. We received messages from all over the world from intercessors such as our district pastoral officials, many pastor friends around the country, and even the intercessors at Hillsong Church in Australia. We did everything we could. We asked students from a local Christian university to come over to our home for an evening of worship and prayer. We were quoting scripture. I was sleeping with a prayer shawl, watching videos, doing natural remedies, and even eating properly. Our whole life became a life of faith and wellness like no other time in our lives. We made no room for doubt or negative talk. It wasn't like we were trying to impress God, but we did not want to have any regrets. So we did everything we could to fight.

One time my husband walked into our bedroom late at night and found my iPad on next to me and a video of Reinhard Bonnke playing. It was a crusade from Africa, and many were being healed in this crusade. But I fell asleep, and the iPad was still playing! That was the kind of commitment we made to our healing. And two months into this journey, we were training our mind, preparing our home, disciplining our bodies with the right nutrition, and fasting and praying for a miracle. That God would use this moment in our life to inspire many people.

In late October, about three months after the diagnosis, we had a big test that would give us an update of our setting. We had been going through weekly exams and blood tests since the diagnosis, but this was a major moment for us. Aside from being nervous, we were very excited. Because we knew we were not alone. The weekend before the test, we had students over to our home for prayer and fasting and to anoint me with oil before this test. These were the closest students to us at the time. And that night was special. *Actually Jane did more of the ministry that night to the students as she prayed for many of them and their situations. Several students told me that they were blown away by her selflessness that evening by praying for them.*

The following Tuesday morning, after the prayer meeting that weekend, we had our blood test and doctor's appointment. The nurse told us that we would get a call in a few hours. That afternoon, I received the call from the doctor's office. Jeff was home that day attending to me, and I brought him over to the phone. These were the words we heard from our doctor. The PET scan has shown "no evidence of recurrent or residual disease." Those were the exact words on the printout that we received also.

My cancer had gone from 71 percent melanoma in my bone marrow to 0 percent. We had just received a complete bone marrow biopsy, PET scans, and blood work. And each of these showed no internal lesions and zero cancer in the bone marrow. Not only did God heal me of the DIC blood disorder that should have taken my life, the cancer went from 71 percent to 0 percent, and the bone lesions disappeared! I believe God healed me and was giving me a chance to tell my story.

My LDH enzyme level that shows the energy and life level in the blood and determines the spread of cancer was over eight thousand just days before. Now, after all of the initial treatment, nutrition, discipline, and prayers, it became normal and in the range of 150 to 250. They had rarely seen anyone with numbers as high as mine drop so quickly. And now they were back to normal. One doctor said that this certainly wasn't solely the chemo we had been taking because we were not taking it long enough; nor was this an aggressive short-term treatment dose. It was prescribed to us for long-term management and systemic treatment targeted at symptoms to slow tumor development. But this was a miracle. My doctor even called me her "Miracle Girl."

Jeff Continues the Story

Just reading Jane's thoughts makes me so very grateful to have experienced an obvious move of God and a miracle in our lives. Over the next nine to ten months, we would enjoy great health. We regained strength and were back to normal with our routines and schedules. And we even shot a short-story video with our church that posted our journey. At one point, the video had received more than twenty-eight thousand views. As Jane recovered so quickly, we would enjoy watching our grandson born in

December, traveling and sharing her story through the entire winter and spring, and walking in that healing and condition for the next ten months. It was a ride that convinced us that God was not done with Jane; He was using this situation to define her dash, both for us as a family and to everyone who was watching us.

Our family was going through a hardship that took every ounce of trust, wisdom, strength, and obedience we had. And one of the comforts in the journey was this verse from Psalms that became a constant reminder. I used this often to model to the young people around us about how to go through hardship. The verse was in Psalm 71.7 and 18 and says, "My life is an example to many because you have been my strength and my protection…let me proclaim your power to this generation, your mighty miracles to all." We cannot go through this without sharing our struggle with this generation.

> Our prayer was that one hundred thousand teenagers will come to Christ through our family trial. What a powerful thought. The brokenness of the generation that we served for over thirty years together became so real to us now. It was now personal, my broken palace.

People could watch what we were going through and be drawn to Christ and find help in their situation. We need an adjustment in our thinking in America when we go through hardship. It is important that we think correctly and stop becoming the delicate and entitled snowflakes this generation has become. At some point in life, when hardship hits the palace, we have to respond by allowing God to redeem the trials in our life. That is exactly what we did. We asked God to redeem hardship in our life. And that is what He did. We were living out Psalm 71 and showing everyone around us how to go through hardship. It was imperative that we did this. Everything was going to change again in our life, unexplainably and shockingly.

The Second Diagnosis

On Friday, July 10, 2015, early in the morning, about eleven months after her first diagnosis, Jane woke me up. We were at a youth camp speaking that week and had just completed the last service the night before on Thursday evening. We stayed up that night and talked about all of the great things that happened at camp and fell asleep in perfect peace. We would sleep in, get up Friday morning, and head home the next day.

Early in the morning, she woke me up and said to me, "I cannot move my left leg." I was exhausted from the week of ministry and had a word of wisdom for her. I told her to simply change her position, that her leg had fallen asleep. And like the wise and concerned husband that I am, I went back to sleep. But just a few minutes later, she woke me again and could not move her left side. I got up and came around to her side, and she was almost completely paralyzed on her left side. And she was in the middle of a stroke.

I immediately called 911. And then I called the camp directors, who were our close friends. They helped me take Jane and our belongings immediately to the ED near the camp, where she began getting tests. While she was in testing, I called our doctor, who had been the lead on our team, and explained to her what was going on.

She told me, "Jeff, get Jane to Minneapolis immediately. I'll meet you at the hospital."

Because we were two hours away and Jane had worsened while in the ED, we decided to take her in the ambulance to Minneapolis in case she worsened. I couldn't take care of her while driving.

After arriving in Minneapolis and following a series of tests in the ED that Friday afternoon, our doctor gave us the news that Jane had developed tumors on her brain and had a stroke. She was admitted and was in the hospital again for the next twenty-three days. And everything became eerily similar to the previous time we were in the hospital, only with even less hope being given to us this time. While in the hospital the second time, Jane would develop tumors throughout her body and be given another short life span of just a few weeks by the same doctors who had cleared her just months before.

We had fought through the first diagnosis and were enjoying sixteen months of health, to live and enjoy each other again and to create more ministry and memories that we thought we would never get a chance to live. But now we would be faced with the worse news. Even though Jane's physical body was changing again, nothing had changed in our spiritual lives. We attacked this second diagnosis with the same kind of faith and determination we had in the first diagnosis. We increased our prayers, disciplines, and everything else we were doing previously.

And God began to do an even deeper spiritual work in each of us and in our family, as He was preparing us for the toughest moments of our life, for the final moments of our life together. And we had a choice to make. We do not always choose our circumstances. But we always choose our attitude and our response.

A Second Fight

And yet even at the most difficult time, with all of the reminders around us such as doctors, nurses, the hospital cafeteria, countless trips back and forth from the hospital and home, medications and machines, and well wishes from thousands of people, our faith could not have been stronger. In these few weeks in the hospital, I would see my children begin to minister to us like never before. Obviously they had a faith of their own, but now they were exercising their faith and showing Jane and me what they were made of in ways unseen until now. It was amazing to see them in the hospital room or observe them pushing Jane in rehab or caring for her by serving her in whatever way she needed it. To see their fight, their humor, their determination, their selflessness, and their faith in action made our fight much easier. Not easy, but easier.

After a few weeks, she was fitted for a wheelchair, and we were sent home. During the next four months, all of our relationships would change as we came together as a family and fought for another healing in Jane's body. There was no weakness or submission, and we still determined to not have end-of-life discussions. It was all trust and faith that God was going to do it again. We would see another healing and enjoy many years together—more grandchildren, the marriage of our youngest son, and many more years of youth ministry. We were defining our dash with perseverance and faith. There wasn't any room for anything else in our mind.

Making Sense of the Senseless

Repeating many of the same disciplines as before, we spent the next four months believing for the same result, healing in Jane's body. You might be thinking that, if we believe God healed Jane the first time, why would she be sick again? How could God do that? Are you sure she was healed? Let me answer that clearly.

First, there was no doubt from anyone involved in Jane's case that she was healed. Jane was healed and reversed what was diagnosed over her. And medical tests and records showed the facts of her initial healing. And she was given another lease on life after the first diagnosis.

Second, I was reminded during the second diagnosis that every person Jesus healed in the Bible died after He healed them. Remember, even Lazarus died after Jesus raised him. Even Jairus's daughter died after Jesus healed her. It is God who gives life and takes breath. Jane would pass into life with Christ when He was finished with her, whenever that was. And it is our responsibility to define the dash in the life we have left, however long that is.

Third, we simply asked God and believed in Him for healing. How He chose to do that was not up to us. It was up to Him. And we were okay with that. We were okay with the months of life we enjoyed between the diagnoses and the way we walked until her death. And we were okay with the completion of her purpose on earth also.

Fourth, we saw the effects of the healing on Jane over the course of that first year. The doctors said the same thing. Remember, they called her "Miracle Girl." We saw it in her body as she continued her life without affect and limitation, and we saw the effect upon many people who were watching us. God was receiving the glory from such a difficult situation.

Finally, and let me be clear, I believe that healing takes place in two settings: both in the here and now and the ever after. We were able to see both of these types of healing

Furthermore, let me explain one more thing I believe. This was all senseless. We cannot understand everything. And it is important for us to know this. We do not need to understand everything. The scriptures say that we "see through a glass dimly now, but then, we will see clearly, as face to face." I believe that God granted us a year with her that we were not supposed to have. He was giving us some sense to deal with this and to show others how to go through hardship. We believe that God strengthened, matured, and sustained us and went through everything with us.

The scriptures we had read and memorized together still meant something to us. The prayers and the songs were still upholding us. We continued attending church and events and had our public dates just like we had done before. We were not living in denial. We were living in demand. We were living in desperation. We believed that our prayers so moved God that He could do nothing but give her to us for that year. Why? To fulfill everything she needed to fulfill in God's time and to define her dash. And so that I could write this book for you to read. To find strength in your situation.

It's all about perspective. You can look at the second diagnosis and be discouraged. Or you could look at it this way. He extended our marriage so we could get to know each other under circumstances that we had never been through in an even greater way. He extended our marriage so we could watch our children grow up and become stronger believers. So we could enjoy the birth of our first grandchild, travel and minister to thousands of people, and make more memories that are still very important to us today. He gave us that year of healing so we could be an example to thousands of people around us and show them how to go through hardship, suffering, and pain. He gave our family the year with her because He loved us. Did you hear that? Because He loved us. We all have a choice to make in hardship. We do not always control our situation, but we always control our attitude. What will your choice be?

Our Final Days
As the final days drew near, the weekend of Thanksgiving was very special to us. Jane was in the wheelchair exclusively, and her condition was worsening so we had Christmas 2015 during Thanksgiving. On the Monday following Thanksgiving, she would slip into a coma and then pass away on December 18. Those four weeks taught us many lessons. The entire family spent almost all of the last four weeks together serving each other, praying for each other, and believing until the final hours. We never had end-of-life discussions up to this point.

Let me explain why that was so important to Jane and me. Jane loved her life and did not want to die. So we decided we would fight. Likewise, I did not want Jane to pass away. So I determined to fight personally so I would have no regrets by doubting that God was going to heal her. I had no room for doubt. I made no room for concession. We would challenge each other to only believe. Knowing my makeup, it was important for me to keep our faith so, if she did pass away, I could look myself in the mirror and know I did everything possible. Even when she couldn't speak her faith, I spoke it for her. So she and I decided that we would only have faith conversations.

And I would deal with her death alone if it were to happen. And that's exactly what I did. I have dealt with her death with God directly, then my family, and now even some of my closest friends. I needed that. And because of the way we decided to handle this, I have no regrets.

While she was in a coma, I would read and sing to her and serve her as if she were still very much alive and responding to me. Each morning I would ask God to heal her so we could dance again and the kids could talk to her once more. And when it didn't happen, I would continue on my day, serving her and speaking, singing, or reading to her. I would also take care of ministry or family business or talk with the family. Each of the family would take their turns sitting with or speaking to her or praying with her and serving her. I know that many conversations were had between the kids, my family, and her parents and family who were all there for so long Every evening I would read to her from her prayer blanket she slept with. It had verses of healing all over it, and we memorized many of them together as we read them. And each night I would read the scenes of heaven from the book of Revelation in the New Testament. And I would commit her to God, asking Him to take her if He wanted to. She was only a gift to me for a short time while here on earth. And we would pray, sing, and hold hands each night as we fell asleep. And the next morning I would repeat it all over again.

Defining The Dash

On the night before Jane went into a coma, we knew it was her last moments. And we decided to talk about eternity, heaven, our life together, the kids, and ministry. I made a mistake to bring up the fact that, if she passed, I was going to pray for a miracle one more time. She was not really happy about that and told me not to. It was then she told me that she was done and that God was finished with her. I disagreed with her and told her that God was not done with her and we had more to do. But that didn't work. She told me that I had work to do, but she was finished with what God had called her to. I could see it in her eyes. She had one foot in heaven and one foot on earth. She had fulfilled everything in her dash that she was supposed to do.

We truly do not believe that it was cancer that took her life. It may have caused her death, but it did not take her life. She lived her life, her dash, beyond what most others could fit into a hundred years. And sickness did not win. It cannot win if we fulfill everything that God has called us to. It can bring death, but sickness cannot take life. If we are winning at life, we cannot lose at death!

I'm not thinking about what I've lost. I'm thinking about what I found. See, some people never find what I lost. I had thirty-four years with Jane. Some people never get a year with that kind of person or that kind of love. I'm not thinking about what life could be like if she were here. I'm thinking about how profoundly she changed my life while she was here. I'm not thinking about how God let me down. I'm thinking about how close to God that I am today because of all of this. If I'm going to trust God in the good times, then I'm going to trust Him in the bad times. I'm not thinking, *Where are you, God?* I know exactly where He is. I see Him in the healing and the hardship with us.

See, Jane was born in 1962. And God gave her a dash to live, to define the time she had left, however much that is. The average person will live about seventy-six years. But what we do with those years is what is most important. And Jane defined her dash the way God had told her she should. That is the essence of life. What are you doing with your dash? With the time you have left? Why are you taking up space, showing your face, and running this race? We do not lose if sickness, an accident, or natural causes bring our death. We lose if we don't fulfill our dash or if we don't make the number of years we have been given count. No, these things cannot take life. Jane has her life. Cancer did not take that. God got everything out of her that He wanted. Purpose and sovereignty took her life. And you have your life right now. Do not let anything take that from you until God is finished with you

Eighteen days after she went into a coma, she completed everything she had to do on this earth. On December 18th, 2015 she won. And our family would continue on from that day forward with so many lasting conversations and memories of an incredible mother. And on that day I would say good-bye to my best friend. I had lost what many people never find. But I have never forgotten a very important lesson I learned through this whole journey. **If we are winning at life, we cannot lose at death.**

I was speaking to a fourteen-year-old girl from Las Vegas. She was telling me how broken her family was. Her mother was a prostitute and wanted her to do the same. But she came to this youth convention and gave her heart to Christ. This fourteen-year-old would not be another statistic of a generational curse. She would be the first Christian in her family. As we talked, I felt everything she was going through.

I'm not so sure that I could have had conversations with teenagers like I have had the past two years if I had not gone through this hardship. It changed the way I have conversations with teenagers and, for that matter, with God. It has given me the ability to communicate with them on their level more than at any time in my ministry.

And just like I am winning in my hardship, this fourteen-year old from Las Vegas is winning as well. That weekend would be the most important two days in her life. Why? I received a note from the youth pastor only a couple weeks after the youth convention. The young girl, who had given her life to Christ at the convention, was killed in a car accident just days afterward. But she will spend eternity in heaven.

#ifjobhadtwitter Since hardship & trial are seen in Christianity & scripture, why are we upset that they are seen in Christians & culture?

CLOSING

*Nothing in life, including human suffering,
comes without a purpose.*

—John Calvin

Job teaches us some very important lessons about suffering and hardship, mainly that it happens to all of us and is a universal blessing in disguise, no matter our family upbringing, financial situation, religious background, age, race, or gender. We need to unlearn that suffering and hardship are a negative thing, that suffering and hardship are a curse upon someone because of his or her doing, and that suffering and hardship are to be avoided at all costs. And Job also taught us that we should unlearn that it is okay to blame God or others for suffering and hardship when it does come. Maybe much of the hardship we are going through is our own fault.

The correct perspective is that we should be thanking Him in everything. Not for everything, but thanking Him *in* everything. One of the great lessons we can learn about suffering and hardship is that it serves a valuable purpose in our lives. To have the right perspective of hardship will assure that we will not waste it when it does come to us.

What else have we learned in these pages? A theme of brokenness and ruin are present in culture and scripture that contrasts how we think in America today. And the simple most valuable lesson we can learn is to un-learn a few things we have been taught along the way. We are to rethink the place of hardship, suffering, and trial in our lives and redeem it. Pop psychology may say that "I'm okay; you're okay," and pop music might boast "Because I'm Happy," but the reality is that we are not okay. And we are not happy. All have sinned and fallen short of the expectations of God. If we admit this, Christ is faithful to forgive us of our sin and cleanse us from unrighteousness. If we do not admit this, the wages of our sin are death. In fact, not just ultimate eternal death, but the kind of death in life many are living right now. And only God can forgive us of our sins.

God is very comfortable with our hardship. He does His greatest work in the midst of our greatest need. Darkness does not intimidate Him. I knew God did not bring me to this point in life to leave me. We serve a God who goes through it with us. His presence and peace never left Job or me. I knew He was in control, and I never doubted Him because His presence was so real in the mess that it was going to be easy to create a message out of all of this.

On Hardship

So to close out this book, I want to give you a reference chapter, a quick review of the book in two sections. First, we need to commit to memory the scripture verses on hardship so we are not simply facing hardship, suffering, and pain with our own words or with what culture says about it. And second, I want you to see a quick reference of the personal lessons I learned. I don't think that I could have written some things two years ago, at least not with certainty or experience. With all of the practicality of this chapter, maybe you could have just read this closing and not the rest of the book!

The Bible on Hardship

Without emphatic and absolute truth, our framework for measuring principle is shifting. I prefer an authoritative unbending and dependable truth structure and not a personal bending and relative truth structure. Can there really be any kind of integrity and consistency in relativism? For example, if every driver of a vehicle decided that his or her age, experience, car type, and schedule dictated the speed limit, we would be in trouble.

So to that end, here is the truth structure for our lives. Please enjoy a very practical way to add truth to your situation. When you mix your thoughts with the Bible, you will guarantee yourself with a win.

Isaiah 43.1–3

"Do not fear, for I have redeemed you; I have summoned you by name; you are mine. When you pass through the waters, I will be with you; and when you pass through the rivers, they will not sweep over you. When you walk through the fire, you will not be burned; the flames will not set you ablaze."

Proverbs 14.12–13

"There is a way which seems right to a man, but its end is the way of death. Even in laughter the heart may be in pain, And the end of joy may be grief."

Psalm 7.7 and 18

"My life is an example to many because you have been my strength and my protection…let me proclaim your power to this generation, your mighty miracles to all."

Ecclesiastes 3.1 and 11

"To everything there is a season, and a time for every purpose under heaven; a time to be born, a time to die…a time to kill, and a time to heal…a time to weep and a time to laugh, a time to mourn and a time to dance…a time of war and a time of peace. And He has made everything beautiful in its time."

John 16.33

"I have told you these things, so that in me you may have peace. In this world, you will have trouble. But take heart! I have overcome the world."

Luke 17.12–19

"As he was going into a village, ten men who had leprosy met him. They stood at a distance and called out in a loud voice, 'Jesus, Master, have pity on us!' When he saw them, he said, 'Go, show yourselves to the priests.' And as they went, they were cleansed. One of them, when he saw he was healed, came back, praising God in a loud voice. He threw himself at Jesus' feet and thanked him—and he was a Samaritan. Jesus asked, 'Were not all ten cleansed? Where are the other nine? Has no one returned to give praise to God except this foreigner?' Then he said to him, 'Rise and go; your faith has made you well.'"

Romans 8.18–25

"I consider that our present sufferings are not worth comparing with the glory that will be revealed in us…That the creation itself will be liberated from its bondage to decay and brought into the freedom and glory of the children of God. We know that the whole creation has been groaning as in the pains of childbirth right up to the present time. Not only so, but we ourselves, who have the first-fruits of the Spirit, groan inwardly as we wait eagerly for our adoption to sonship, the redemption of our bodies. For in this hope we were saved. But hope that is seen is no hope at all. Who hopes for what they already have? But if we hope for what we do not yet have, we wait for it patiently."

Romans 16.20

"And the peace of God, which transcends all understanding, will guard your hearts and your minds in Christ Jesus."

2 Corinthians 1.4–7

"God, who comforts us in all our troubles, so that we can comfort those in any trouble with the comfort we ourselves receive from God. For just as we share abundantly in the sufferings of Christ, so also our comfort abounds through Christ. If we are distressed, it is for your comfort and salvation; if we are comforted, it is for your comfort, which produces in you patient endurance of the same sufferings we suffer. And our hope for you is firm, because we know that just as you share in our sufferings, so also you share in our comfort."

2 Corinthians 4.7–10
"But we have this treasure in jars of clay to show that this all-surpassing power is from God and not from us. We are hard pressed on every side, but not crushed; perplexed, but not in despair; persecuted, but not abandoned; struck down, but not destroyed. We always carry around in our body the death of Jesus, so that the life of Jesus may also be revealed in our body."

2 Corinthians 11.24–28
"Five times I received from the Jews the forty lashes minus one. Three times I was beaten with rods, once I was stoned, three times I was shipwrecked. I spent a night and a day in the open sea. In my frequent journeys, I have been in danger from rivers and from bandits, in danger from my countrymen and from the Gentiles, in danger in the city and in the country, in danger on the sea and among false brothers, in labor and toil and often without sleep, in hunger and thirst and often without food, in cold and exposure. Apart from these external trials, I face daily the pressure of my concern for all the churches."

Philippians 3.10
"That I may know Him, His death, His resurrection, and the fellowship of His suffering."

Hebrews 12.5–8, 11
"My son, do not make light of the Lord's discipline, and do not lose heart when he rebukes you, because the Lord disciplines the one he loves, and he chastens everyone he accepts as his son. Endure hardship as discipline; God is treating you as his children. For what children are not disciplined by their father? If you are not disciplined—and everyone undergoes

discipline—then you are not legitimate, not true sons and daughters at all. No discipline seems pleasant at the time, but painful. Later on, however, it produces a harvest of righteousness and peace for those who have been trained by it."

James 1.2–4
"Consider it pure joy, my brothers and sisters, whenever you face trials of many kinds, because you know that the testing of your faith produces perseverance. Let perseverance finish its work so that you may be mature and complete, not lacking anything."

Revelation 22.2–5
"On each side of the river stood the tree of life, bearing twelve crops of fruit, yielding its fruit every month. And the leaves of the tree are for the healing of the nations. No longer will there be any curse. The throne of God and of the Lamb will be in the city, and his servants will serve him. They will see his face, and his name will be on their foreheads. There will be no more night. They will not need the light of a lamp or the light of the sun, for the Lord God will give them light. And they will reign for ever and ever."

Grenell on Hardship
Aside from the scriptural practicality of this book, let's look at some of the key moments of the book in review. I want you to remember some of the things after reading this book. I know how powerful phrases can be. Hopefully these phrases will be easy for you to remember when you go through hardship and suffering. I want you to enjoy a very practical review of the key moments in the book for me. To close the book, I want to include some of my personal lessons learned through this entire experience.

- "You will never be able to avoid the storms of life, but you will always be able to dance in the rain."
- "Every athlete knows the value of pain, but not every person knows the value of pain."

- "God has a very different view of hardship, suffering, and trial than we do. And we must adjust our thinking of suffering to His thinking and our view of hardship to His view."
- "God always has a say in the end of the story."
- "Our problem with hardship is that we do not see the big picture or the ending, and we get stuck in the smaller moments of suffering."
- "Our perspective of our problems as Americans is based upon elitism that will not allow hardship or suffering into our palace."
- "Christianity embraces hardship as a tutor to greater character and ultimately spiritual maturity."
- "Hardship is where God does His best work. Hardship does not intimidate God. In fact, God does His greatest work in the midst of our greatest need."
- "We are God's Magnus Opus, His greatest work. He places our chaos on His canvas and creates His greatest masterpiece."
- "We live in a broken palace, but God is the landlord."
- "The degree to which you utter praise to God in the midst of your hell is directly related to the presence of God that will be with you in the midst of your hell."
- "People who have gone through brokenness can become great examples and help others who may be going through it."
- "The faith of the church is for the fears of the world."
- "If we are going through a hardship or trial, we are assured of two things. First, we are His child. And second, He will be with us."
- "Nothing is too difficult for Him, and nothing is too simple for Him."
- "When it comes to having an answer for suffering and hardship, sometimes our answer is simply, 'I don't know.' And that's okay."
- "You should never go through hardship alone."
- "We see through the glass dimly now, but there will be a time when the glass will be totally clear and we will be able to see clearly."
- "Our concept of God, suffering, and hardship should be taken from the scriptures and not from culture."

- "Our view of God is vital to our response to hardship. Reading through scripture is a lesson on who God is and how He uses hardship to shape someone. Reading through culture is a lesson on who God is not and how He uses hardship to punish someone."
- "Life just happens sometimes, and it is nobody's fault."
- "If we are winning in life, we cannot lose at death."
- "God is playing chess (several steps in front of us), and we are playing checkers (merely looking at the next step in front of us)."
- "If you want a degree in spiritual maturity, you must graduate from the University of Suffering."
- "Every palace has steeples and gardens, jesters and dragons, and princes and princesses who grow up to be kings and queens who slay dragons."
- "If you are going through hardship or discipline, you are a son or daughter. If you are not going through it, you are a bastard and without a parent or family."
- "Most people will choose to focus upon the pain in their life. But I have chosen to focus upon the presence in my life."
- "I had great friends until they opened their mouth. The presence of friends is sometimes more important than their words."
- "Sometimes I do not control my situation or the outcome. But always I control my attitude."
- "When it comes to hardship, time doesn't heal. What we do with our time heals."
- "If things are bad, it is not the end. Because in the end, things will not be bad."
- "God may not be the cause of my hardship and suffering, but He is there because of my hardship and suffering."
- "People often ask, 'Where is God in all of this?' I say, 'He is with you in the midst of it.'"

Made in the USA
Columbia, SC
22 February 2018